Very best wishes

Scala

AUDUBON

The Charleston Connection

Edited by
Albert E. Sanders and Warren Ripley

With a foreword by
John Henry Dick
and
Photographs by
William A. Jordan

From the Charleston Museum Exhibition
8 September — 17 November 1985

Contributions from the Charleston Museum
XVI

Table of Contents

Preface

This book is intended to serve as a document of the Charleston Museum exhibition entitled "Audubon: The Charleston Connection," which was on public view from 8 September through 17 November 1985 in commemoration of the 200th anniversary of the birth of the creator of the monumental *Birds of America.*

With a unique assemblage of original works, prints, artifacts, manuscript material, and rare ornithological specimens, the museum presented a three-dimensional essay on the life and contributions of John James Audubon and, especially, his association with the Charleston naturalist John Bachman. The story of these men and their families is a magnificent saga set against the panorama of a changing America preoccupied with westward expansion and internal problems that would lead to the explosion of civil war. Audubon did not live to see his beloved America torn asunder, but Bachman did; and, like many others in the South, he suffered grievously from it. But that is another part of the story. It is with the Audubon years that we are concerned here as we pause to reexamine this extraordinary man, who was fortunate enough to see the great American wilderness before it was reduced by expansionism.

During the 1830s Charleston, South Carolina, was Audubon's second home. As he observed, some of the happiest moments of his life were spent under the Bachman roof poring over specimens of birds and mammals with John Bachman, working on his paintings for the plates in his splendid *Birds of America,* and instructing Bachman's talented sister-in-law, Maria Martin, in the techniques of watercolor painting that he used to capture his avian subjects so vividly. It is not surprising that he enjoyed the durable old city so much, because Charleston was good to John James Audubon. It gave him his staunch friend and advisor, John Bachman, wives for his two sons and a friendly haven to which he could retreat from the snipings of his detractors. Of the latter, he was not without his fair share.

Partly because of some ill-considered statements that he had made in a talk before the Academy of Natural Sciences of Philadelphia in 1824, and partly because his work threatened to eclipse the accomplishments of the pioneer ornithologist Alexander Wilson, Audubon had incurred the dislike of the well-to-do Philadelphia naturalist George Ord, who had carried Wilson's *American Ornithology* to completion after Wilson's death in 1813. Ord and the eccentric English naturalist Charles Waterton branded Audubon a charlatan and published blistering attacks upon his credibility. In his unusual position as the only person who had collected birds with both Wilson and Audubon, John Bachman recognized the merits (and faults) of both men, so when he came to Audubon's defense he did so with dignity and without denigrating Wilson. His wisdom is evident in his letter to Audubon of 25 March 1835:

> "Do not trouble yourself about your opponents — never answer them, your friends will do that for you — Go on with your work and prosper — it may leave you poor in purse but rich in fame. Men may talk of their Wilson (I mean the Philadelphians) did they not neglect him while living although they now wish to build him a monument when he is dead. I could give them an inscription; for I saw him dying by inches with poverty, neglect and mortification."

The vitriolic Ord was not devoid of fairness and had great respect for Bachman's abilities despite his friendship with Audubon. "You have taken the proper course, Reverend Sir; you listen to all; but you examine for yourself; and report the result only of your own investigations. ... I rejoice that the subject has fallen into the hands of one so fully competent," he wrote to Bachman on 26 May 1837 in acknowledgment of a paper that Bachman had submitted for publication by the Philadelphia Academy — a paper in which Bachman had courteously discredited one of Ord's previous publications.

The high regard in which Bachman was held by his contemporaries clearly made him a valuable ally for Audubon. But Bachman was an equal beneficiary of their friendship, his youthful interest in natural history having been rejuvenated by Audubon's first visit to Charleston and their subsequent ventures into the field for specimens for Audubon to paint. Devoted to his congregation at St. John's Lutheran Church, the minister-naturalist denied himself the pleasure of accompanying Audubon on his distant collecting trips, settling for vicarious enjoyment of the adventures that Audubon recounted in his letters to the Bachman household. But occasionally this noble man would betray what must have been a deep longing to be a part of Audubon's exploits. "Oh how I wish I were with you," he wrote in a letter to Audubon prior to the latter's departure on a collecting trip to Maine in 1832.

Audubon spent entire winters with the Bachmans and was thus exposed to the wise counselings of his friend for extended periods. The jovial Bachman gave him constant encouragement, bolstering his sagging spirits with humor and the promise of immortal fame when *The Birds of America* was at last completed. At times the end of that enormous project seemed almost unattainable, and Audubon often had doubts that he would live to finish it. It was at such times that Bachman's friendship was particularly valuable. Out would come the chess board, and Bachman would entice Audubon to lay aside his brush or pen for a pleasurable diversion from his rigorous schedule of painting and writing. Audubon then could vent his frustrations on Bachman's chess pieces, and apparently did so with the same degree of skill that he laid down a wash with his watercolor brush. With a cozy fire crackling on the hearth and a glass of claret at his elbow, the vagabond artist could let his mind escape into the complexities of the game.

Forgotten for the moment were the humiliation of bankruptcy at Henderson, Kentucky, the houndings of his creditors, the derisive comments of George Ord and his adherents, and, above all, the relentless pressure to sell subscriptions to *The Birds of America.* Without that income there was no money to send to Lucy and the boys and no money with which to buy the French brushes and paints that he preferred or the fine English paper on which his glorious birds came to life. If he could not sell enough subscriptions on a continuous basis, Robert Havell could not be paid to engrave the plates or to pay his colorists to finish the prints. And if those demands could not be met, all was lost.

Unsuccessful in his earlier business ventures, Audubon had gambled his family's future upon his ability to produce a large and expensive work on the birds of America. The financial success of the enterprise would depend, ironically, upon his salesmanship and management of the funds received. He had saddled himself with tremendous responsibilities, and at times they terrified him almost to the point of panic. It was then that he was assailed by the "blue devils," as he called his feelings of depression.

But there was little room for devils of any color in the Reverend Bachman's home; his mirthful blue eyes and ready laugh would quickly chase them away, and Audubon could snugly lose himself in a chess game as the rain pattered down outside on a chilly December evening in Charleston. Passersby, hurrying through the gloom to the warmth of their own firesides, might briefly notice the dimly lit ground floor windows of the Bachman home, but they could not know that behind the drawn curtains sat a man who was destined to be recognized as one of the truly great artists of his time.

Across from him was the sturdy Lutheran minister whose contributions to his friend's greatness may never be completely known or fully appreciated. But Audubon knew what he owed John Bachman and expressed his gratitude to him many times in his *Ornithological Biography.* Together, they would win dual fame as producers of the classic *Viviparous Quadrupeds of North America,* to which Audubon lent his magic brush and Bachman his careful pen. That arduous venture was the culmination of their years of friendship but also was Audubon's last effort.

Reminiscent of his fears about *The Birds of America,* Audubon did not live to see the *Quadrupeds* completed. His sons, Victor and John, filled the void — as best they could — and helped Bachman through to the final pages. Although the seemingly endless demands of the work would at times strain the Audubon-Bachman family friendships to their limits, they bent but did not break. At last the *Quadrupeds* was finished, but Audubon was not there to savor the moment. "Old Jostle," as Bachman had dubbed him, was gone. He had blazed across John Bachman's life like a comet, and Bachman would remember the pleasures of those years until he died.

Albert E. Sanders
Curator of Natural Sciences
The Charleston Museum
Charleston, South Carolina
January 1986

Foreword

The importance of John James Audubon in American art and his place in the affections of the American people grow with the years.

With a flair for the dramatic, Audubon carried a dagger and gun into the wilderness, wore long hair and dressed in buckskin. He possessed the instincts of a red Indian and the cultivation of a French aristocrat.

He always retained a strong feeling and understanding of the living bird but he was foremost an artist. He broke away from the stilted, mounted creations of his predecessors and, by using wires, posed his freshly collected models into positions often with an oriental flair.

A sizeable portion of Audubon's success should be shared with his talented London engraver, Robert Havell, Jr. Together they had the courage to use Double Elephant size plates, 29½ x 39½ inches, so that even the largest of birds would be depicted life size. This was the most imposing format ever attempted up to then in the history of book publishing. The results are legend.

John James Audubon has become a national hero, a legendary figure beloved alike by conservationists, a growing army of bird watchers and a troubled generation searching for its heritage.

John Henry Dick

Acknowledgments

We wish to thank the following individuals and institutions for loans of items to our exhibit, *Audubon: The Charleston Connection:* W. Graham Arader III of Philadelphia; Edward Kenney of Washington, D.C.; Teresa Farris of the College of Charleston Foundation, and Oliver Smalls of the Robert Scott Small Library, College of Charleston; the Charleston Library Society; Charles Duell and Sarah Lytle of the Middleton Place Foundation; David Wright of the Pierpont Morgan Library; and Dr. Frank Sommer of the Winterthur Museum.

Particular thanks are due to twelve private individuals who, together, lent the bulk of the items that appeared in the exhibit and who have chosen to remain anonymous. We regret that we cannot publicly recognize each of them. They opened their collections to us without reservation, and we are deeply grateful.

Photographs of items in their collections were provided by Hildegarde Stephans of the American Philosophical Society; Linda Snow of the John James Audubon Museum; Mary Alice Kennedy of the New York Historical Society; Donna McCombs of the Pierpont Morgan Library; Dr. Frank Sommer of the Winterthur Museum; and William Cuffe and Caroline Rollins of the Yale University Art Gallery. We are indebted to the owner of the Audubon self-portrait (page 15) for permitting us to publish a photograph furnished by Helen Sanger of the Frick Art Reference Library. We also thank Michael Marsland for taking a critical photograph in another city, Dr. Anne C. Hanson for permitting us to publish Victor Audubon's portrait of Eliza Bachman, and the Rev. Edward L. Counts of St. John's Lutheran Church who furnished the photograph of John Bachman's residence.

We are especially grateful to Peter Manigault and the Charleston Post-Courier Foundation for contributing a large portion of the exhibit costs and for the contribution of funds for restoration of four important paintings in the Charleston Museum collections in time for them to be included in the exhibit (pages 35, 39, 70, 97). The Post-Courier Foundation also has made a generous contribution toward the cost and production of this volume. Another important contribution toward the the expenses of the exhibit was made by an anonymous donor in memory of Ellison A. Williams, a prominent amateur ornithologist in the Charleston area for many years.

Most of the photographs in this volume are the result of the fine photographic work of William A. Jordan, whose services were made possible by the Post-Courier newspapers. It also gives us great pleasure to acknowledge the assistance of Ray Holsclaw, of Carolina Prints and Frames of Charleston. His cheerful donations of time, services and materials were major contributions. We also thank Charles Thompson for the custom-made wood letters of the exhibit title panel.

We had originally intended to include eight color plates in this volume. Due to the generosity of five donors, however, we were able to include sixteen. The persons who contributed to the increased quality of the catalogue are Merle H. Sparkman, Henry Fair, John Henry Dick, Howard Burky, and Dr. Thomas Gaffney. Mr. Burky and Dr. Gaffney are both members of the Charleston Museum Board of Trustees of which Dr. Gaffney is president.

In conclusion we wish to extend our appreciation to the noted bird artist John Henry Dick and to Peter Manigault and Arthur M. Wilcox of the Post-Courier for serving on our Audubon Exhibit Committee, which was rounded out by Albert E. Sanders, Curator of Natural Sciences. If we have failed to mention someone to whom thanks are due, it is only because so many contributed to the exhibit and made this volume possible. To everyone we express our most sincere gratitude.

John R. Brumgardt, Director
The Charleston Museum

EDITOR'S NOTES:

The format of a book is considerably different from that of a museum exhibition. Consequently, the order of appearance of certain items in the exhibit, *Audubon: The Charleston Connection,* has been altered in the interests of narrative continuity. However, all items and label text of the exhibit are included in this volume and have been enhanced by the addition of supplementary material on pages 31, 53, 54, 84, 105, 125, 126, 128 and 131.

As a matter of record, we call attention to four original works by John James Audubon that are published here for the first time (pages 13, 16, 17, 100). We also are pleased to include seven previously unpublished works by John Woodhouse Audubon (page 48), Victor Audubon (pages 34, 53), George Lehman (page 51), and Maria Martin (pages 70, 75, 76). A watercolor sketch, probably attributable to John Woodhouse Audubon, is on page 50. A fifth original by John James Audubon, "Woodchucks," his watercolor study for Plate 2 of the *Quadrupeds of North America,* is published in color for the first time in our Plate 4.

JOHN JAMES AUDUBON
1785 — 1851

Oil on canvas by his son,
John Woodhouse Audubon, c. 1841

"The man ... was not a man to be seen and forgotten. ... The tall and somewhat stooping form ... the steady, rapid, springing step, the long hair, the aquiline features, and the glowing, angry eyes — the expression of a handsome man conscious of ceasing to be young, and an air and manner that told you that whoever you might be he was John Audubon, will never be forgotten by anyone who knew or saw him."
ANONYMOUS, 1868, LONDON *Athenaeum*

SEE PLATE 1, Page 133

Private Collection

**SHOTGUN USED BY
JOHN JAMES AUDUBON
c. 1835**

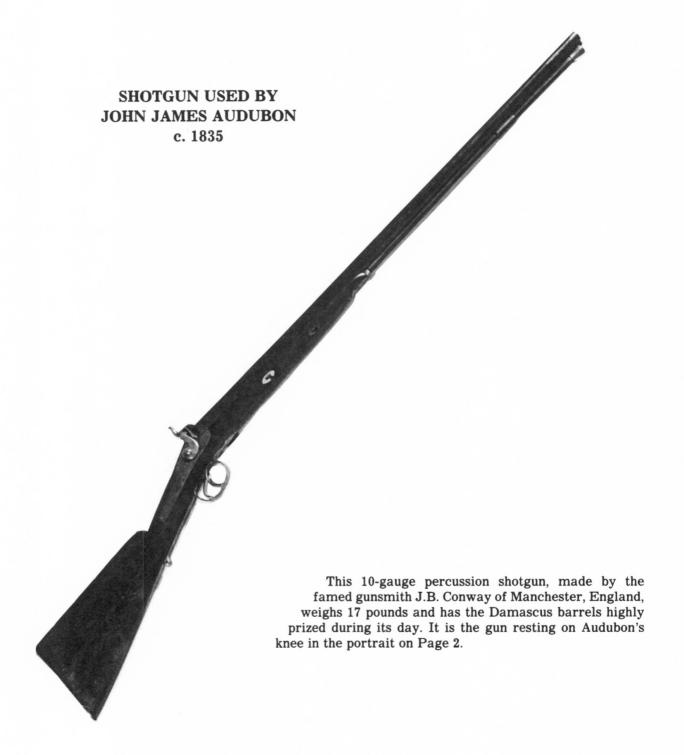

This 10-gauge percussion shotgun, made by the famed gunsmith J.B. Conway of Manchester, England, weighs 17 pounds and has the Damascus barrels highly prized during its day. It is the gun resting on Audubon's knee in the portrait on Page 2.

Private Collection

"He had the advantage of being a foreigner ... so that he took nothing for granted, and ... all things American struck him as fresh. He had the further advantage that he was a genius, and a genius of art at that, so to observe, to depict what he saw, was habitual and instinctive."
DONALD CULROSS PEATTIE, *Audubon's America*

"His simplicity, tremendous vitality, enthusiasm for life in all its variety, and his drive for creative excellence made him one of the most enduring personalities in American history."
ROGER TORY PETERSON, *The Art of Audubon*

The Formative Years

Les Cayes

Jean Jacques Audubon, later Anglicized to John James, was born 26 April 1785 on the island of Santo Domingo at his father's plantation near Les Cayes, Haiti. Audubon never knew his mother, Jeanne Rabine, who died the following November at the age of 27.

When slave unrest began to threaten French-colonial rule of Santo Domingo, his father, Jean Audubon, a French naval and merchant marine officer, sold his plantation and returned to his home near Nantes, France. In 1791 he sent for his six-year-old son and his daughter Rosa to join him in France.

JEAN AUDUBON
1744 — 1818

Father of John James Audubon
Oil on canvas, artist unknown

Attained the rank of lieutenant in the French Navy. While commanding a corvette with the French fleet under Count de Grasse, he witnessed the surrender of the British at Yorktown in 1781.

In 1772 he married the widow Anne Moynet, who became a devoted stepmother to the young John James Audubon.

"My father and I were of the same height and stature, say about five feet ten inches, erect, and with muscles of steel; his manners were those of a most polished gentleman."

AUDUBON, "Myself," *Audubon and His Journals*

Private Collection

MILL GROVE FARM
Near Valley Forge, Pennsylvania

From an oil by Thomas Birch, 1830s

In 1789 Jean Audubon purchased this 280-acre farm on a tributary of the Schuylkill River northwest of Philadelphia.

In 1803 he sent the 18-year-old John James here partly to remove him from the threat of conscription into Napoleon's army and partly in hopes that he would learn English.

"Mill Grove was ever to me a blessed spot. ... Hunting, fishing, drawing and music occupied my every moment; cares I knew not, and cared naught about them."

AUDUBON, "Myself," *Audubon and His Journals*

Photo courtesy of the New York Historical Society

7

PHOEBE
Sayornis phoebe (Latham)

At Mill Grove the young Audubon began to draw the birds that he saw and to observe their habits, as he had done as a youngster in France.

In a cave on the farm he became fascinated with a pair of nesting phoebes. To see if their offspring would return to the same cave the following year, he "fixed a light silver thread to the leg of each, loose enough not to hurt the part, yet so fastened that the birds could not remove it."

This experiment appears to be the first attempt at banding birds in the United States.

Charleston Museum Collections

LUCY BAKEWELL AUDUBON
1786 — 1874

From a miniature by Frederick Cruickshank, c. 1834

On the estate next to Mill Grove Audubon met Lucy Green Bakewell in 1804 and married her there on 5 April 1808.

The young couple set up housekeeping in Louisville, Kentucky, where Audubon and Ferdinand Rozier, son of a friend of Jean Audubon, had established a store.

From copy in private collection. Photo courtesy of owner.

ALEXANDER WILSON
1766 — 1813

From an oil by Rembrandt Peale

A Scot, Wilson wrote and illustrated the first comprehensive account of North American birds. His *American Ornithology,* published between 1808 and 1814, earned for him the title of "Father of American Ornithology."

Wilson passed through Louisville in 1810 seeking specimens and subscriptions for his book. He stopped in Audubon's store but failed to interest him in a subscription.

Seeing Wilson's work, Audubon realized that his own paintings of birds were better. This discovery seems to have inspired him to undertake the great work of his life — to paint the birds of America.

Photo courtesy of The American Philosophical Society

10

A GROWING FAMILY

VICTOR GIFFORD AUDUBON
Born, Louisville, Kentucky
12 June 1809

JOHN WOODHOUSE AUDUBON
Born, Henderson, Kentucky
30 November 1812

From oils by John James Audubon, 1822

Photos courtesy of The John James Audubon Museum, Tyler Collection.

AUDUBON'S MILL, HENDERSON, KENTUCKY

In 1810 the Audubons moved farther down the Ohio River to Henderson, Kentucky, where they met with disastrous financial reverses, the worst of which was the failure of a steam mill built in 1817 by Audubon and Lucy's brother, Thomas Bakewell, "at an enormous expense."

"... the building of that accursed steam mill was of all the follies of man, one of the greatest ... and misfortune after misfortune came down upon us. ... I parted with every particle of property I held to my creditors ... and at last left Henderson ... without a dollar in my pocket."
AUDUBON, "Myself," *Audubon and His Journals*

PORTRAIT OF A YOUNG WOMAN
Possibly Anne Bakewell Gordon,
Sister of Lucy Audubon

Pencil and black chalk on paper by John James Audubon, 1824

Drawn "In 30 minutes" (notation in unidentified hand)

"My plantation in Pennsylvania had been sold, and ... nothing was left to me but my humble talents. ... I undertook to take portraits of the human 'head divine,' in black chalk, and succeeded admirably.

"... My drawings of birds were not neglected meantime; in this particular there seemed to hover round me almost a mania, and ... I thought that I now drew birds far better than I had ever done before. ..."
AUDUBON, "Myself," *Audubon and His Journals*

Private Collection

DOWN THE MISSISSIPPI

In October 1820 Audubon left his family in Cincinnati and set out on a flatboat down the Ohio and Mississippi Rivers, intent on enlarging his collection of bird paintings. Accompanying him was his gifted young pupil Joseph Mason (1807-1883). Although only 13 years old, Joseph was producing splendid botanical drawings that Audubon began using as backgrounds for his birds. Already considering some kind of publication of his works, Audubon promised Joseph that his name would appear on the plates.

Existing at the poverty level, they painted the birds and plants that they saw on their way, barely supported by the sale of Audubon's black-chalk portraits and their hunting. In August 1822 Joseph finally became disillusioned and left Audubon in Louisiana to return to his home in Cincinnati. However, he left in Audubon's hands some of the finest botanical illustrations ever produced in America.

JOHN JAMES AUDUBON, 1823

From a self-portrait in oil

By 1824 Audubon had become determined to publish his paintings in a grand work on the birds of America. However, his penniless wanderings in the wilderness had temporarily cost him his family, which Lucy now supported by teaching school in Louisiana.

At last rejoining them there, "with rent and wasted clothes and uncut hair," as he put it, Audubon convinced Lucy that he would have to seek a publisher in England. Largely through her efforts, they had managed by the end of 1825 to save nearly $1,700 for his trip.

"Without her zeal and self-sacrificing devotion, the world would never have heard of Audubon."
                    FRANCIS H. HERRICK, *Audubon the Naturalist*

Private Collection. Photo courtesy of the Frick Art Reference Library.

CHAFFINCH
Fringilla coelebs Linnaeus

Watercolor on paper by John James Audubon, Edinburgh, 1839

At New Orleans on 17 May 1826, Audubon boarded the ship *Delos* for Liverpool, England.

"In his portfolio he had all the material he needed to continue working for many months. Some of his pictures were ... ready for the engraver; some he had once considered finished but now realized should be done over; some were merely sketches on which he could base future pictures. In addition, he had his notes on birds because ... he hoped to publish a text to accompany his illustrations."

ALEXANDER B. ADAMS, *John James Audubon*

Private Collection

CHUCK-WILL'S-WIDOW
Caprimulgus carolinensis Gmelin

Oil on canvas by John James Audubon, before 1839.

Copy of original watercolor painting for Plate 52, *The Birds of America*, by John James Audubon. The snake is the Eastern Coral Snake, *Micrurus fulvius.*

Playing his role as the self-styled "American Woodsman," Audubon brought a sense of American frontier adventure to his English hosts. His confidence soared, and on 6 August 1826 he noted in his journal, "I am well received everywhere, my works praised and admired, and my poor heart is at last relieved from the great anxiety that has ... agitated it, for I know now that I have not worked in vain."

SEE PLATE 2, Page 134

Private Collection

17

WILD TURKEY
Meleagris gallopavo Linnaeus

Plate 1, *The Birds of America,* by John James Audubon.

The first 10 plates of *The Birds of America* were engraved by William H. Lizars of Edinburgh, Scotland. The remaining 425 were the work of Robert Havell, Jr., of London.

"The great size and beauty of the Wild Turkey, its value as a delicate and highly prized article of food, and the circumstances of its being the origin of the domestic race now generally dispersed over both continents, render it one of the most interesting of the birds indigenous to the United States of America."

AUDUBON, 1831, *Ornithological Biography,* Vol. I

Private Collection

YELLOW-BILLED CUCKOO
Coccyzus americanus (Linnaeus)

Hand-tinted engraving by Mark Catesby.

Opposite Page 9 of Catesby's *Natural History of Carolina, Florida and the Bahama Islands*, Vol. I, London, 1731.

With the financial support of twelve prominent men in England and America, the artist-naturalist Mark Catesby spent the years 1722-1725 in Charleston gathering specimens and making sketches and observations for this two-volume work. Published in London in 1731 and 1743, these richly-illustrated folios were the most ambitious treatment of North American flora and fauna attempted in the 18th century. Many of Catesby's South Carolina specimens are preserved today in the British Museum (Natural History).

Catesby's figure and account of the "Cuckow of Carolina" were the basis for Linnaeus' description of this species in 1753. Handpainted in watercolors by Catesby himself, this figure is somewhat stilted by modern standards, but no moreso than many other bird illustrations of the 18th century.

Charleston Museum Collections

YELLOW-BILLED CUCKOO
Coccyzus americanus (Linnaeus)

Figure 1, Plate 28, *American Ornithology*, by Alexander Wilson, Vol. 4, 1811

This classic work was the first attempt to describe and illustrate the birds of the United States.

Wilson's figures of birds were far better than those of Catesby, showing much greater accuracy in form and markings. However, they lacked the life-like quality that Audubon gave his birds, as Wilson had noticed in the paintings he saw in Audubon's store the year before this volume was published.

After Wilson's death in 1813 the ninth and final volume of his *Ornithology* was completed and published in 1814 by George Ord, an influential member of the Philadelphia Academy of Natural Sciences. Viewing Audubon as a competitor and a threat to Wilson's memory, Ord attempted to discredit him as a reliable ornithological observer but was finally overwhelmed by the sheer magnitude of Audubon's accomplishments with *The Birds of America* and his *Ornithological Biography*.

Charleston Museum Collections

YELLOW-BILLED CUCKOO
Coccyzus americanus (Linnaeus)

Plate 2, *The Birds of America*, John James Audubon

"The branch, among the foliage of which you see the male and female winging their way, is one of the Papaw, a tree of small size, seldom more than from twenty to thirty feet in height."

AUDUBON, 1831, *Ornithological Biography*, Vol. I

This excellent botanical study is the work of young Joseph Mason. The realism of the plant and Audubon's active birds is almost startling in comparison to the stiffly-posed figures by Catesby and Wilson, neither of whom possessed the true artistic genius that Audubon had been refining since childhood.

He had achieved his success in painting birds by wiring the subject in the desired position onto a board marked off in squares and then outlining its form on the board, giving careful attention to the exact measurements of the bird. The result was a highly accurate, life-sized image that Audubon then reproduced in watercolor.

"I am sorry that some of my friends ... are against the pictures being the size of life," Audubon noted in his journal on 24 November 1826, "... but my heart was always bent on it and I cannot refrain from attempting it."

Private Collection

21

My Style of Drawing Birds —

When ~~yet~~ I first began ~~my attempts~~ of representing Birds on paper, I was ~~not~~ far from possessing much knowledge of their Nature, and like hundreds of others ~~who~~ the object was put aside under the Idea that if was completing by the possessing of some bird of a back and tail — ~~Too little for in lieu of Legs~~, and other four to supping the ~~not generalise bird~~, I was twaddling myself with the thoughts that statements ~~might have been much~~ in ~~the preventing~~ their falling backward of forward were still requisite to insure the appearance of proper gravitation — and so ~~which~~ bills and claws I did ~~produce~~, ~~without speaking~~ both were of a straight line for a back and a tail stuck in beyond the natural rumps like an caustiffing Rudder —

Those persons who ~~beheld~~ my father saw my ~~miserable~~ attempts were ~~fairly~~ to praise them to the Skies, and no one was perhaps ever more likely to be completely smoked than I ~~and~~ by those false affections — My father however taking my different to me — he constantly assuring one that nothing in the world possessing life and animation was easy to imitate, and that as ~~I grew older he hoped~~ I would become more and more afraid of this — he was so kind to me in every thing unconnected with my mental improvement, that to have desired to listen to him with speaking seriously would have been highly ungrateful, and his maxims becoming laws at it were, I listening less to others, more to him and ~~you~~ slowly improved —

The first collection of Drawings I made of this sort were from European specimens procured by my father or myself, and I still have them in my possession — My own all representing ~~strictly ornithologically~~ which means neither more or less than in stiff ~~and unfeelingly~~ profiles, such as are found in all works published since the beginning of the present century. — My work for was begun in America, and there without any knowledge or mentor I betook myself to the drawing of specimens hung to a string by one foot with the desire to show their very position as the wings leg body though as well as the tail — in this manner I made some tolerably fair Egg Drawings for Paultising!

One day while watching the habits of a pair of Pewees at Milligrove I looked so intently on their innocent attitudes, that a thought struck my ~~mind~~ like a flash of light, that nothing after all could one autumn my authentic desire to represent nature, than to attempt to copy her in her own way. ~~Seeing alive and Moving!~~ — Thus, as I went with prancing hundreds of outlines of my favourites, how going or bad I cannot tell, but I fancied I had mounted a step on the high Mount before me — I continued for months together in simply watching birds as I observed them either alighting on one wing leg easily with some of my sketches. — I procured many individuals of differing species and laying them on my table or on the ground tried to place them in such attitudes as I had sketched, but alas they were dead to all intents and variations — a living thought came to my assistance — by means of thread I hang some thing like Wing or a Tail and by fastening the threads securely I had something like Wing or a Tail and by fastening the threads securely — when I saw the living bird alive before me, yet much was wanting — what I saw the living bird self the blood rose to my temples and almost in despair spent a long Month without drawing, but in deep thought and daily in the country of the feathered inhabitants of Dear Will Grove. — I had drawn from the Mauskin which under David and have obtained tolerable figures of our species through this means, and regatted him far a manikin of a bird would answer for all of them, and labouring in wood and with wires, and ~~forming a grotesque figure~~ which I cannot decent in any other terms than by ~~nameing just what it was~~ "a doll" a very tolerable looking Dado" a living ~~pigeon~~ laughed heartily and asking my blood by ~~affecting~~ one, that as for me as to represent a Dear Pewee or bird of that ~~but~~ my model at night with to represent a Dear Pewee or bird of that ~~but~~ my model would do — I gave it a kick, demolished if to atoms any wishing ~~it~~ and beginning again —

Young as I was, my impatience to obtain my desired felling my brains with differing plans — may I not unfrequently dreaming that I had made a new discovery, and long before day, on morning I leaped out of bed fully persuaded that I had obtaining my object —

"MY STYLE OF DRAWING BIRDS"
By John James Audubon

First page of the original manuscript of an episode written in Edinburgh, Scotland, in 1831. On a later page Audubon wrote:

"The more I understood my subjects the better I became able to represent them in what I hoped was a natural position. The Bird once fixed with wires on squares ... I studied it whilst thus placed as a 'lay figure' before me ... this led me to judge ... of its general form, of those of its bill, nostrils, head, eye, legs or claws, as well as the structure of its Wings and Tail — nay the very tongue was at times of importance to me, and I thought that the more I understood of all those particulars, the better representations I made of the originals. If successful or not, I leave for you to decide."

The published version, edited by William MacGillivray, appeared in Audubon's *Ornithological Biography*, Vol. IV, 1838.

Courtesy of W. Graham Arader III Galleries, Philadelphia.

ORNITHOLOGICAL BIOGRAPHY,

OR AN ACCOUNT OF THE HABITS OF THE

BIRDS OF THE UNITED STATES OF AMERICA,

ACCOMPANIED BY DESCRIPTIONS OF THE OBJECTS REPRESENTED
IN THE WORK ENTITLED

THE BIRDS OF AMERICA,

AND INTERSPERSED WITH DELINEATIONS OF AMERICAN
SCENERY AND MANNERS.

BY JOHN JAMES AUDUBON, F.R.SS.L.& E.

FELLOW OF THE LINNEAN AND ZOOLOGICAL SOCIETIES OF LONDON ; MEMBER OF THE LYCEUM
OF NEW YORK, OF THE NATURAL HISTORY SOCIETY OF PARIS, THE WERNERIAN NATURAL
HISTORY SOCIETY OF EDINBURGH ; HONORARY MEMBER OF THE SOCIETY OF NATURAL
HISTORY OF MANCHESTER, AND OF THE SCOTTISH ACADEMY OF PAINTING, SCULPTURE,
AND ARCHITECTURE ; MEMBER OF THE AMERICAN PHILOSOPHICAL SOCIETY, OF THE
ACADEMY OF NATURAL SCIENCES AT PHILADELPHIA, OF THE NATURAL HISTORY SOCIETIES
OF BOSTON, OF CHARLESTON IN SOUTH CAROLINA, &c. &c.

VOL. III.

EDINBURGH :

ADAM & CHARLES BLACK, EDINBURGH ;

LONGMAN, REES, BROWN, GREEN & LONGMAN, LONDON ; R. HAVELL,
ENGRAVER, 77. OXFORD STREET, LONDON ; THOMAS SOWLER,
MANCHESTER ; MRS ROBINSON, LEEDS ; ALEXANDER HILL, EDIN-
BURGH ; J. HENRY BEILBY, BIRMINGHAM ; E. CHARNLEY, NEW-
CASTLE-UPON-TYNE ; AND GEORGE SMITH, LIVERPOOL.

MDCCCXXXV.

THE ORNITHOLOGICAL BIOGRAPHY
Volume III, 1835, by John James Audubon

Text for *The Birds of America*. Published in five volumes from 1831 to 1839.

"I shall publish the letterpress in a separate book, at the same time with the illustrations, and shall accompany the descriptions of the birds with many anecdotes and accounts of localities connected with the birds themselves, and with my travels in search of them."
AUDUBON, European journals, 24 November 1826. *Audubon and His Journals*.

Here, five years before publication of the first volume, Audubon stated the exact plan that he followed with the text for his *Birds of America*. In preparing it, he secured the help of one of Britain's most capable naturalists:

"I feel pleasure in here acknowledging the assistance which I have received from ... **Mr. WILLIAM MAC-GILLIVRAY** who ... has aided me ... in completing the scientific details and in smoothing down the asperities of my Ornithological Biographies."
AUDUBON, 1831, *Ornithological Biography*, Introduction, Vol. I.

Charleston Museum Collections

24

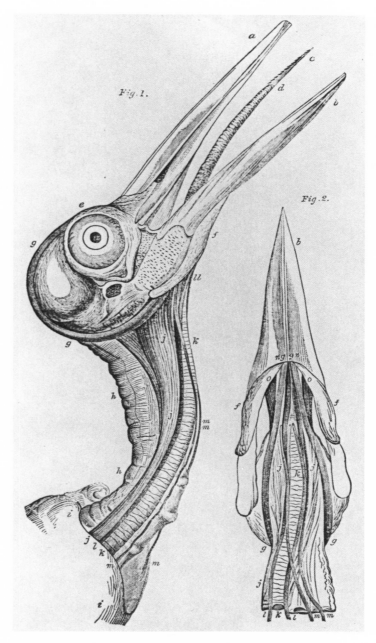

IVORY-BILLED WOODPECKER
Dissection of head and neck

Ornithological Biography, Vol. V, Page 528

Although greatly overshadowed by the plates in *The Birds of America,* the figures and descriptions of the internal anatomy of many American birds are among the most valuable features of Audubon's *Ornithological Biography.*

"These anatomical descriptions and the sketches by which they are sometimes illustrated, have been executed by my learned friend **WILLIAM MACGILLIVRAY**. ..."
                    AUDUBON, 1838, *Ornithological Biography,* **Introduction, Vol. IV**.

Charleston Museum Collections

ORIGINAL COPPER PLATE USED TO PRINT "THE MARSH TERN"
Gull-Billed Tern, *Sterna nilotica* Gmelin

Plate 410, *The Birds of America*, by John James Audubon. Engraved by Robert Havell, Jr.

The image of Audubon's "Marsh Tern" is reversed and very faint in this copper engraving used by Havell to print Plate 410 in the Double Elephant Folio of *The Birds of America*. Havell's plates are considered to be among the finest examples of the aquatint method of engraving, a process whereby tonal areas, rather than lines, are etched into the copper with acid to achieve variations of shading.

Havell mastered the difficult process almost to perfection and skillfully combined it with etching and line engraving to capture the soft shading of feathers and foliage as well as the strength of the bolder features of Audubon's paintings.

Fewer than 100 of the original copper plates survive today. Many were melted as scrap metal about 1873.

Stamped into the reverse side of this plate is the name and address of one of Havell's suppliers of blank copper plates: "W^M HIAM ... 9 JOHNS ROW ... BATH S^T ... CITY R^D ... LONDON." Fries (1973, *The Double Elephant Folio*, p. 395) notes "A. Hian, 9 Ratcliff Road, Bath Street, City Rd." and "Pontifex and Stiles, 23 Lisle Street, Soho, London" as the two other known suppliers.

Private Collection

UNCOLORED PRINT OF "MARSH TERN"
Gull-Billed Tern, *Sterna nilotica* Gmelin

Plate 410, *The Birds of America*, by John James Audubon

When completed, the copper plate was inked and black-and-white impressions were printed. This print, struck from the copper plate on Page 27, shows the subtle gradations of tone that Havell achieved with the aquatint method.

A single wash of watercolor laid down over an area of these graded tones produced corresponding changes in the tone of that color, thereby reducing the amount of detailed shading required by the colorist and insuring greater uniformity of color tones from one print to the next.

Private Collection

COMPLETED PRINT OF "MARSH TERN"
Gull-Billed Tern, *Sterna nilotica* Gmelin

Plate 410, *The Birds of America,* by John James Audubon

Havell "colored the prints in the usual manner by flowing washes of pure water-color tints over the monochrome proof which was printed from the copper plate. In this phase of the process the great charm of his genuine talent for water-color painting asserted itself. Aside from the first crude washes, put on by artists or colorists employed for the purpose, he himself applied the salient tones and all the more delicate tints."
GEORGE A. WILLIAMS, 1916, *Print Collectors Quarterly*

With an enthusiastic determination equal to that of Audubon, Havell carried the production of *The Birds of America* to completion without any serious complications. It now seems quite unlikely that any other engraver of his time could have accomplished this enormous task in such masterful fashion.

Private Collection

THE BIRDS OF AMERICA
Double Elephant Folio
By John James Audubon

Vol. I of four volumes published in London, England, between 1827 and 1838

"This work, comprising four hundred and thirty-five plates, and one thousand and sixty-five figures, was finished on the 20th of June 1838, without the continuity of its execution having been broken for a single day, and the numbers having been delivered with exemplary regularity; for all of which I am indebted to my friend and Engraver, Mr. Robert Havell."

AUDUBON, 1838, *Ornithological Biography,* **Vol. IV**

"The sumptuous character of this work, its commanding beauty, as well as its surprising accuracy, considering all the obstacles of time and circumstance, mark it, ... with its letterpress, as one of the most remarkable and interesting undertakings in the history of literature and science in the nineteenth century."

FRANCIS H. HERRICK, *Audubon the Naturalist*

The work was issued in 87 parts, each consisting of five unbound plates. Subscribers paid $1,000 for the complete set of plates and the five volumes of text.

Between 175 and 200 complete sets of the Double Elephant Folio were produced. The exact number is not known.

Courtesy of The Robert Scott Small Library at The College of Charleston

MOCKING BIRD
Mimus polyglottos (Linnaeus)

Plate 21, *The Birds of America*, by John James Audubon

"The mellowness of the song, the varied modulations and gradations, the extent of its compass, the great brilliancy of execution, are unrivalled. There is probably no bird in the world that possesses all the musical qualifications of this king of song, who has derived all from Nature's self."

AUDUBON, 1831, *Ornithological Bioography,* **Vol. I**

Courtesy of The Robert Scott Small Library at The College of Charleston

JOHN JAMES AUDUBON

From a miniature by Frederick Cruickshank, c. 1834

Private Collection. Photo courtesy of the owner

"I have grown up in the school of adversity and am not an unprofitable scholar there, having learnt to be satisfied with providing for my family and myself by my own exertions ... I know I am engaged in an arduous undertaking; but if I live to complete it, I will offer to my country a beautiful monument of the varied splendor of American nature, and of my devotion to American ornithology."
AUDUBON TO G.W. FEATHERSTONEHAUGH, 7 December 1831

"I doubt if I should ever have had the stamina to work as he had to; I should have failed to stem the tide of adversity — and I know I could never, in his time or mine, have negotiated the great folio reproduction and its attendant enormous financing. What a monumental thing for a reed bent by the faintest breath of emotion, as he was, to have accomplished.

LOUIS AGASSIZ FUERTES

The Charleston Connection

VIEW OF CHARLESTON FROM THE HARBOR

From an oil by S. Bernard, 1831

In August 1831 Audubon returned to America as a well-known figure, having published the first volumes of *The Birds of America* and the *Ornithological Biography*. Needing more subscribers and more birds from the Southeast, Audubon undertook a trip down the Atlantic coast toward Florida, taking with him the artist George Lehman, to paint backgrounds for the birds, and a young English taxidermist, Henry Ward. Leaving Washington, D.C., in mid-October of 1831:

"We at length approached Charleston, and the view of that city across the bay was hailed by our party with unfeigned delight. Charmed ... with having terminated our ... journey, it did not occur to us to anticipate the extraordinary hospitality which awaited us there, and which led to ... a few of the happiest weeks I ever passed."

AUDUBON TO G.W. FEATHERSTONHAUGH, 7 December 1831

Photo courtesy of Yale University Art Gallery

JOHN JAMES AUDUBON

Miniature by Victor Audubon, c. 1840

Oil on Ivory. *Private Collection*
(Copied from an 1835 engraving by Robert Havell of
the Cruickshank miniature, Page 31)

JOHN BACHMAN

Portrait by John Woodhouse Audubon

(Oil on canvas, page 39)

"I had passed but one night in the city, when I was presented to the Rev. Mr. Bachman. ... When I first saw this excellent man he was on horseback, but upon my being named to him, he leaped from his saddle ... and gave me his hand with a pressure of cordiality that electrified me."
AUDUBON TO G.W. FEATHERSTONHAUGH, 7 December 1831

"Mr. Bachman! Why, my Lucy, Mr. Bachman would have us all to stay at his house ... Could I have refused his kind invitation? No! ... We removed to his house in a crack — found a room ready for Henry to skin birds — another for me and Lehman to draw in and a third for thy husband to rest his bones in on an excellent bed."
AUDUBON TO LUCY AUDUBON, October 1831

BENNETT'S MILL POND

Oil on canvas by Henry Jackson, c. 1840

On their way to John Bachman's house Audubon and his assistants passed this scene on Rutledge Avenue two blocks south of the Bachman residence. It was a familiar sight to Bachman, who passed it on his way home from pastoral duties at St. John's Lutheran Church on Archdale Street.

The pond was filled in during the latter part of the 19th century and in 1899 became the site of the building that housed the Charleston Museum from 1907 until 1979.

SEE PLATE 5, Page 137   *Charleston Museum Collections*

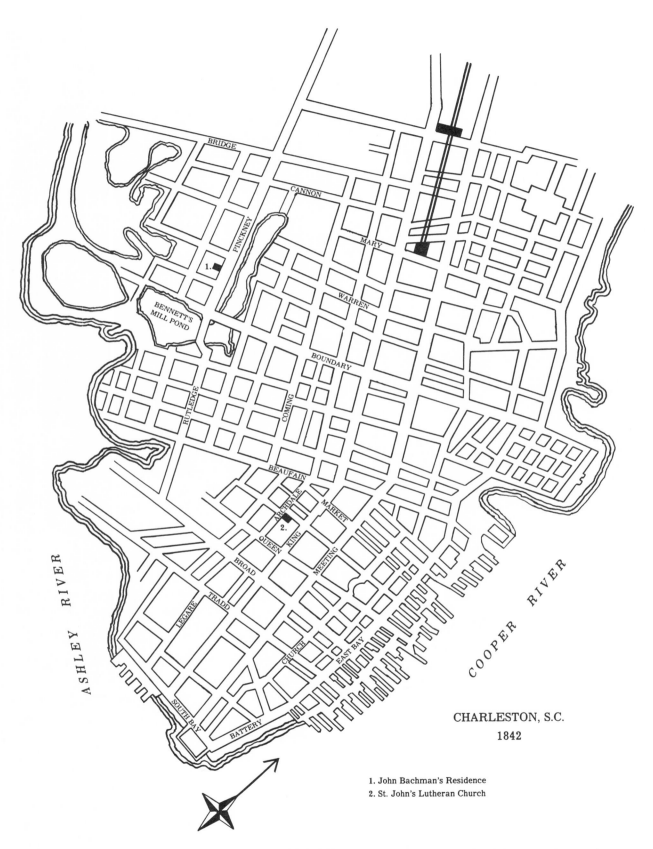

BRIDGE

CANNON

PINCKNEY

MARY

1.

WARREN

BENNETT'S
MILL POND

BOUNDARY

RUTLEDGE

COMING

BEAUFAIN

MARKET

ARCHDALE

2.

QUEEN

KING

MEETING

BROAD

ASHLEY RIVER

LEGARE

TRADD

CHURCH

EAST BAY

COOPER RIVER

SOUTH BAY

BATTERY

CHARLESTON, S.C.
1842

1. John Bachman's Residence
2. St. John's Lutheran Church

Adapted from a map in The Charleston Library Society Collections

JOHN BACHMAN'S RESIDENCE

This Charleston-style dwelling at 7 Pinckney Street (later 149 Rutledge Avenue) was the home of John Bachman, his wife Harriet, her sister Maria Martin and their mother, and the Bachman children, of whom there were always several on hand. Bachman had become pastor of St. John's Lutheran Church on Archdale Street in 1815.

In this turn-of-the-century photograph only weed-grown remnants remain of Bachman's lush garden. When Audubon arrived here in 1831, flowers and shrubs of many varieties flourished in formal beds. A Bachman granddaughter remembered "coral woodbine, dogwood, Cherokee roses — lovely things my grandfather brought from the woods."

Bachman's study was located on the ground floor, and it was there that Audubon painted many of the original watercolors for *The Birds of America.*

The house was demolished in the 1920s.

Photo courtesy of St. John's Lutheran Church

JOHN BACHMAN
1790 — 1874

Oil on canvas by John Woodhouse Audubon, c. 1837

Born in Rhinebeck, Dutchess County, New York, on 4 February 1790, Bachman recalled that "from my earliest childhood I had an irrepressible desire for the study of natural history." He became especially familiar with mammals and birds and went on field trips with Alexander Wilson while in school in Philadelphia in his early teens.

A religious upbringing steered him into the ministry, and he was ordained as a Lutheran minister in 1814. After a trip to the West Indies to recover from a lung hemorrhage, he accepted the pastorate of St. John's Lutheran Church in Charleston, arriving on 10 January 1815. He married Harriet Martin in 1816 and accepted her sister, Maria, and their mother as part of the household. Harriet bore 14 children, five of whom did not survive infancy.

Audubon's visit in 1831 rekindled Bachman's interest in natural history, and he contributed a wealth of information and advice to Audubon in his work on *The Birds of America*. Bachman's concern for accuracy kept the sometimes-hasty Audubon out of hot water on several occasions. With Audubon, and independently, he made notable contributions to the knowledge of North American shrews, squirrels and rabbits and was warmly received by European scientists during his trip to Europe in 1838.

SEE PLATE 6, Page 138   *Charleston Museum Collections*

GREAT BLUE HERON
Ardea herodias Linneaus

Plate 211, *The Birds of America,*, by John James Audubon

"In the Carolinas, where Herons of all sorts are extremely abundant ... on account of the numerous reservoirs connected with the rice plantations ... which contain fish of various sorts, these birds find it easy to procure food in great abundance."

AUDUBON, 1835, *Ornithologhical Biography,* Vol. III

Private Collection

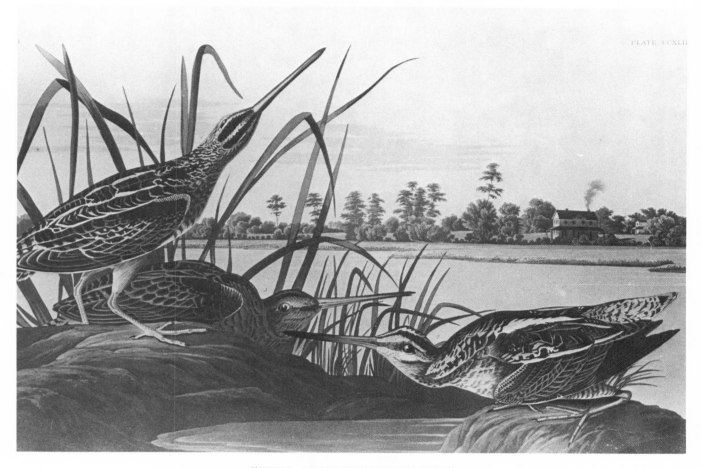

"THE AMERICAN SNIPE"
Wilson's Snipe, *Gallinago gallinago* (Linnaeus)
South Carolina plantation near Charleston

Plate 243, *The Birds of America*, by John James Audubon

"... In South Carolina ... the grounds of the riceplanter afford it abundance of food. In some fields well known to my Charleston friends, as winter retreats of the snipe, it is shot in great numbers. ... In such places I have found these birds by fifties and hundreds in fields of a few acres. ... While traveling eastward from Charleston, in the month of March, I found this Snipe perhaps more abundant near the Santee River than anywhere else."

AUDUBON, 1835, *Ornithological Biography*, Vol. III

SEE PLATE 12, Page 144

Private Collection

BOAT-TAILED GRACKLE
Quiscalus major Vieillot

Plate 187, *The Birds of America*, by John James Audubon

"They are courageous birds, and often give chase to Hawks and Turkey Buzzards. My friend **Dr. SAMUEL WILSON** of Charleston attempted to raise some from the nest ... and for some weeks fed them on fresh meat, but they became so infested with insects that notwithstanding all his care they died.

"In the plate are represented a pair in full spring plumage. I have placed them on their favourite live-oak tree."

AUDUBON, 1834, *Ornithological Biography*, Vol. II

Private Collection

"THE YELLOWSHANK"
Lesser Yellowlegs, *Tringa flavipes* (Gmelin)

Plate 288, *The Birds of America*, by John James Audubon

"I have represented one of these birds on the fore ground of a little piece of water a few miles distant from Charleston in South Carolina, on the borders of which, in the company of my kind friend **JOHN BACHMAN** and others, I have spent many a pleasant hour, while resting after fatiguing rambles in the surrounding woods."

AUDUBON, 1835, *Ornithological Biography,* **Vol. III**

SEE PLATE 13, Page 145

Private Collection

Bachman's Finch

"BACHMAN'S FINCH"
Bachman's Sparrow, *Aimophila aestivalis* (Lichtenstein)

Plate 165, *The Birds of America*, by John James Audubon

"In honoring ... this Finch with the name of **BACHMAN**, my aim is to testify the high regard in which I hold that learned and most estimable individual, to whose friendship I owe more than I can express on this occasion.

"I have represented a male in full summer dress, which was presented to me, while yet quite fresh, by my friend **BACHMAN**.

"The beautiful plant on which it is placed, was drawn by my friend's sister, who has kindly rendered me similar services ... and here let me again express my gratitude toward that amiable lady and her esteemed brother."

AUDUBON, 1834, *Ornithological Biography,* Vol. II

Unfortunately for the honoree, Audubon's name, *"Fringilla bachmanii,"* could not stand because a Georgia specimen of the same bird had already been described as *Fringilla aestivalis* by Lichtenstein in a German publication in 1823.

SEE PLATE 8, Page 140   *Private Collection*

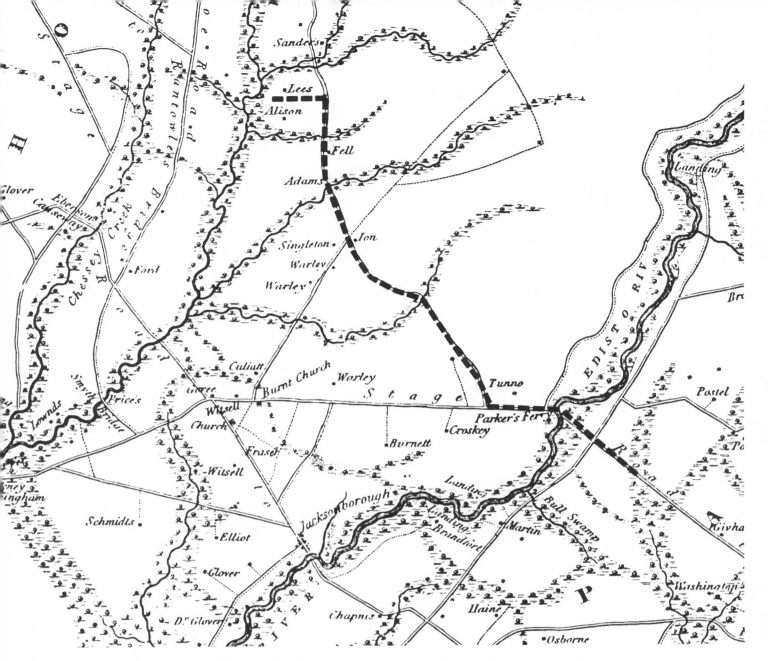

"A SOFT & PLEASANT NOTE THAT WAS NEW TO ME"

The Discovery of Bachman's Warbler

"Now take a seat along side of me and ... go with me over the description & history of this beautiful bird. I have a secret to tell you in your ear, softly my friend, I have the male, it is fairly drawn, it is in full plumage. I have the skin well put up. ...

"I was coming from Maj. Lee's & near Parker's ferry heard a soft & pleasant note that was new to me. ... I saw the bird on the upper branches of the largest Tupelo Tree, I shot it and it lodged in the Moss. Goodbye says I. ... 3 miles further the same sweet note like music from the spheres came over me, I saw and watched the bird for a quarter of an hour, it was slow in its movements keeping very high & occasionally hanging under a limb like the yellow throated warbler. This time I was more successful and the bird is safe. ... The bird I sent you was an old female I thought I had so stated it. ... Now my friend draw this male & female, it will an ornament to your book."

BACHMAN TO AUDUBON, 27 March 1833

The map is from *Mills' Atlas,* Colleton District, 1825.

BACHMAN'S WARBLER
Vermivora bachmanii (Audubon)

Plate 185, *The Birds of America*, by John James Audubon

"My friend **BACHMAN** has the merit of having discovered this pretty little species of Warbler, and to him I have the pleasure of acknowledging my obligations for the pair which you will find represented in the plate, accompanied with a figure of one of the most beautiful of our southern flowers, originally drawn by my friend's sister, **MISS MARTIN**."

AUDUBON, 1834, *Ornithological Biography*, Vol. II

Here, the rarest of all North American warblers is shown with the rarest of the Southeastern shrubs, *Franklinia altamaha,* known in Audubon's day as *Gordonia pubescens. Franklinia* may now be extinct in the wild, and Bachman's Warbler also near extinction.

SEE PLATE 7, Page 139

Private Collection

46

BACHMAN'S WARBLER
Vermivora bachmanii (Audubon)

This specimen (Charleston Museum No. 7614) was collected in Charleston County, S.C., by Arthur T. Wayne on 30 March 1907.

The nest (Charleston Museum No. CBN 66) also was collected by Wayne in Charleston County on 11 April 1917.

After its discovery by John Bachman in 1833 this species was not seen again in South Carolina until Arthur Wayne collected a specimen in Charleston County on 15 May 1901.

MARIA BACHMAN AUDUBON
1816 — 1840

Oil on canvas by John Woodhouse Audubon, Edinburgh, Scotland, 1838

The eldest daughter of John and Harriet Bachman, Maria Rebecca Bachman married John Woodhouse Audubon on 21 June 1837. The youngest son of John James Audubon, John was an accomplished artist in his own right. The marriage strengthened the bonds of friendship between Audubon and Bachman but was tragically short, ending with Maria's death from tuberculosis on 15 September 1840.

"Dear Johnny sends a portrait of myself, which I hope you will all like on the other side of the water as much as we do on this. Many of our friends have seen it and not one yet has pronounced it other than a good likeness and regards the painting, all agree in saying that it is the best and most finished head he has yet done."
MARIA BACHMAN AUDUBON TO MARIA MARTIN, 5 January 1839

Private Collection

JOHN WOODHOUSE AUDUBON
1812 — 1862

From a miniature by Frederick Cruickshank, 1836*

Private Collection. Photo Courtesy of Owner

*The initials "F.C." and date are in the lower right corner of the original.

"FRIENDSHIP ALBUM"
OF
MARY ELIZA BACHMAN
Compiled 1831 — 1836

Watercolor sketch of Carolina Wren, probably by John Woodhouse Audubon, 15 October 1833

Similar to an autograph book, a "friendship album" or "memory book" was kept by many young ladies of the 19th century. It served as a repository for poems, small, pressed keepsakes and good wishes from friends and relatives. This album belonged to Mary Eliza Bachman, second oldest daughter of John and Harriet Bachman.

The fine sketch shown here has been attributed to John James Audubon, but the date "October 15, 1833," suggests otherwise. Audubon's journal shows that on that date he and Lucy were still in Richmond, Virginia, and did not reach Charleston until 24 October. They were greeted by their son, John, who had arrived by steam packet from New York on 12 October and thus is the more likely candidate as the artist of this sketch.

Courtesy of Henry Francis DuPont Winterthur Museum,
Joseph Downs Manuscript Collection No. 66x65

CASTLE PINCKNEY, CHARLESTON HARBOR
Sketch in Mary Eliza Bachman's "Friendship Album"

Watercolor by George Lehman, November 1831

In this excellent little sketch, dedicated to Eliza Bachman, Lehman displays the talents that led Audubon to engage him to paint backgrounds for *The Birds of America.* Lehman did most of the backgrounds for the birds that Audubon painted in Charleston and Florida during the winter of 1831-1832 but parted company with him soon after.

Lehman probably copied this scene from the same sketch that he made for the background of Audubon's painting of the Long-Billed Curlew (page 73) in which Castle Pinckney appears almost exactly as seen here.

Courtesy of Henry Francis DuPont Winterthur Museum,
Joseph Downs Manuscript Collection No. 66x65

VICTOR GIFFORD AUDUBON
1809 — 1860

From a miniature
by Frederick Cruickshank, 1836*

Private Collection.
Photo Courtesy of the Owner

*Date is on backing of framed original.

VICTOR AUDUBON AND MARY ELIZA BACHMAN

Early in 1839 Audubon's eldest son, Victor, visited the Bachmans for the first time, apparently to meet the family of his brother John's wife, Maria. While there he fell in love with Mary Eliza Bachman and the two were married 4 December 1839. Like her sister Maria, Eliza fell victim to tuberculosis and died on 25 May 1841 at the age of 22.

Within eight months John Bachman had lost his two elder daughters, John and Victor their wives, and Audubon his beloved daughters-in-law.

ELIZA BACHMAN AUDUBON
1818 — 1841

From an oil by Victor Audubon, c. 1840

Anne Coffin Hanson. From photo in Charleston Museum Collections

"My lucky star seems to shine brilliantly over me, for though separated for a time from so many dear friends, I am now surrounded by many who use all their endeavours to make me happy and comfortable."

MARIA BACHMAN AUDUBON TO MRS. JOHN M. DAVIS,
London, 24 October 1837

"By this time you will be aware of the indisposition of dear Ria. ... The poor girl has suffered from a sore mouth and a general weakness. ..."

ELIZA BACHMAN AUDUBON TO MRS. JOHN M. DAVIS,
New York, 21 January 1840

"My dear Eliza is better than when I wrote last, and I think will overcome her cold in a week or more, but it has been quite obstinate notwithstanding all we would do."

VICTOR AUDUBON, postscript, ELIZA BACHMAN AUDUBON
TO JANE BACHMAN, New York, 22 March 1840

"John Bachman has told you all that can be said respecting our beloved Maria's situation, and I assure you ... that my last week here has been one of deep sorrow. I go to town and return without scarcely seeing or caring about anyone, and when I return home, it is only to augment the pains of my poor heart."

JOHN JAMES AUDUBON TO VICTOR AUDUBON,
Charleston, 10 May 1840

"I hope ere this you have received my letter to you, which I assure you was written with some exertion. Tell dear Jenny that I intended writing to her to day, but was so much indisposed yesterday that I found myself too weak to attempt it."

ELIZA BACHMAN AUDUBON, postscript, MARIA MARTIN
TO MRS JOHN M. DAVIS, San Pedro, Cuba, 24 January 1841

"Dear Victor
"I do not know that I can add anything that will tend to alleviate your sorrow & comfort you under an affliction that has fallen on you in common with us all. You know our sympathies & we pray God to support you.

Affectionately,
Jno Bachman"

Postscript, JOHN BACHMAN TO JANE BACHMAN,
Charleston, 25 May 1841

"WHITE HERON"
Great Egret, *Casmerodius albus* (Linnaeus)

Plate 386, *The Birds of America*, by John James Audubon

"On foot its movements are as graceful as those of the Louisiana Heron, its steps measured, its long neck gracefully retracted and curved, and its silky train reminded one of the flowing robes of the noble ladies of Europe.

"While traveling, early in spring, between Savannah ... and Charleston ... I saw many of these Egrets on the large rice plantations."

AUDUBON, 1838, *Ornithological Biography,* Vol. IV

Private Collection

WOOD DUCK
Aix sponsa (Linnaeus)

Plate 206, *The Birds of America*, by John James Audubon

"The food of the Wood Duck, or as it is called in the Western and Southern States, the Summer Duck, consists of acorns, beech-nuts, grapes, and berries of various sorts. ... In the Carolinas, they resort under night to the rice fields, as soon as the grain becomes milky. They also devour insects, snails, tadpoles, and small water lizards."

AUDUBON, 1835, *Ornithological Biography,* Vol. III

Private Collection

PLATE CLX

"CAROLINA TITMOUSE"
Carolina Chickadee, *Parus carolinensis* Audubon

Plate 160, *The Birds of America*, by John James Audubon

"My drawing of the Carolina Titmouse was made not far from New Orleans late in 1820. I have named it so, partly because it occurs in Carolina, and partly because I was desirous of manifesting my gratitude toward the citizens of that State, who by their hospitality and polite attention have so much contributed to my comfort and happiness whenever it has been my good fortune to be among them."

AUDUBON, 1834, *Ornithological Biography*, Vol. II

Private Collection

BLACK-HEADED GROSBEAK
Pheucticus melanocephalus (Swainson)

Collected by J.K. Townsend in the Black Hills of South Dakota 3 June 1834. One of the Townsend specimens purchased by Audubon from the Academy of Natural Sciences of Philadelphia in 1836.

Charleston Museum No. 7028

"Now Good Friend open your Eyes! ... Read aloud! ... I have purchased Ninety Three Bird Skins! Yes 93 Bird Skins ... sent from the Rocky Mountains and the Columbia River by Nuttall & Townsend! — Cheap as Dirt too — only one hundred and Eighty-four Dollars. ... Such beauties! Such rarities! ... Ah my Worthy Friend how we will laugh and talk over them!"

AUDUBON TO BACHMAN, 23 October 1836

EVENING GROSBEAK
Coccothraustes vespertinus (Cooper)

"SPOTTED GROSBEAK"
Black-Headed Grosbeak,
Pheucticus melanocephalus (Swainson)

Plate 373, *The Birds of America*, by John James Audubon

"We now proceeded toward Charleston ... and reached in safety the house of my worthy friend the Reverand **JOHN BACHMAN, D.D.** It was indeed a happy meeting! Here I opened the box containing **Dr. TOWNSEND'S** precious series of birds, and ... drew upwards of seventy figures of the species which I had procured at Philadelphia, assisted in the finishing of the plants, branches of trees, and flowers, which accompany these figures, by my friend's sister-in-law, **MISS M. MARTIN**, to whom I now again offer my most sincere thanks."
AUDUBON, 1838, *Ornithological Biography,* **Vol. IV**

NOTE: The males of both species in this plate were taken in the Black Hills by J.K. Townsend on 3 June 1834.

Private Collection

"THE NIGHT HERON"
Black-Crowned Night Heron, *Nycticorax nycticorax,* (Linnaeus)

Plate 236, *The Birds of America*, by John James Audubon

"The Night Heron is a constant resident ... in the low swampy tracts near the coast ... My friend **JOHN BACHMAN** is acquainted with a place on Ashley River, about four miles distant from Charleston, where, among a cluster of live-oak trees, he has for the last fifteen years found a flock of about fifty of these birds during the winter.

"... In some breeding-places near Charleston, which I visited ... with my friend **JOHN BACHMAN**, the nests were placed on low branches, and crowded together. ... Hundreds of them might be seen at once, as they were built on the side of the bushes fronting the water.

"... I have observed it to alight in the ponds in the suburbs of Charleston towards evening, and feed there.
AUDUBON, 1835, *Ornithological Biography*, Vol. III

Courtesy of W. Graham Arader III Galleries, Philadelphia

LITTLE BLUE HERON
Egretta caerulea (Linnaeus)

View Near Charleston, S.C.

Plate 307, *The Birds of America*, by John James Audubon

"My friend **JOHN BACHMAN** informs me, that in South Carolina, this species not unfrequently breeds in the company of the Louisiana Heron, the nest and eggs of which, he adds, are very similar."

AUDUBON, 1838, *Ornithological Biography*, **Vol. IV**

SEE PLATE 14, Page 146

Private Collection

"TURKEY BUZZARD"
Turkey Vulture, *Cathartes aura* (Linnaeus)

Plate 151, *The Birds of America*, by John James Audubon

"The flight of the Turkey Buzzard is graceful compared with that of the Black Vulture. It sails admirably either high or low, with its wings spread beyond the horizontal position, and their tips bent upward by the weight of the body. ... They are more elegant in form than the Black Vultures, and walk well on the ground or the roofs of houses. They are daily seen in the streets of the southern cities, along with their relatives, and often roost with them on the same trees."

AUDUBON, 1834, *Ornithological Biography* **Vol. II**

Courtesy of The Charleston Library Society

THE VULTURE CONTROVERSY

Copy of Published Results of Vulture Experiments, with Inscription by John James Audubon on Cover

From text inside:

"On the 16th December 1833, I commenced a series of experiments on the habits of our Vultures, which continued ... at intervals till the 15th January 1834. ... There were two points on which the veracity of Audubon had been assailed, 1st, Whether the Vultures feed on fresh or putrid flesh, and 2nd, Whether they are attracted to their food by the eye or scent."

JOHN BACHMAN, 1834, *Journal of the Boston Society of Natural History,* Vol. I, pp. 15-31

The experiments seemed to support Audubon's claim that vultures locate their food primarily by sight. The copy is inscribed as follows:

"To Miss Burley with the respectful regards & sincere good wishes of her Humble Servant

John J. Audubon"

Private Collection

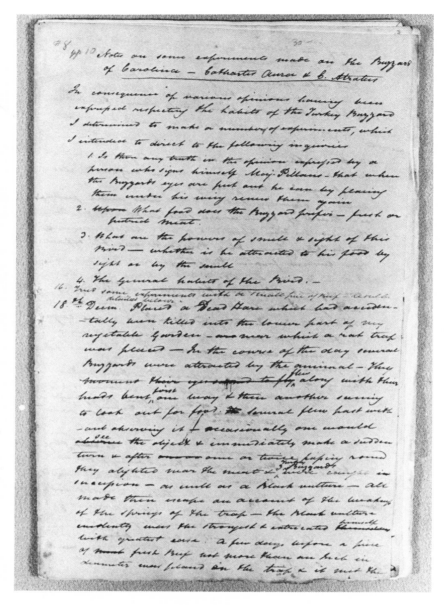

ORIGINAL NOTES RECORDED BY JOHN BACHMAN

During Vulture Experiments in 1833
Conducted in the backyard of Bachman's residence on Rutledge Avenue, Charleston, South Carolina

"22nd Dec.   This was Sunday no experiments tried. ...

"23rd   The meat is becoming offensive — and although the Buzzards have not smelt it, the dogs have. ... Mr. Audubon is this morning painting a sheep under the impression that the buzzards will come to the painting ... it was a coarse affair — on a canvas painted in oil — it represented the animal cut open with his entrails hanging out. In its wet state it was placed in the Garden on the ground. The day was rainy ... & but few Buzzards were flying. The first one ... that made his appearance saw the painting when he was about 70 yards off — gave a sudden turn & alighted near it — walked all round the painting seemed much disappointed — flew off to a point nearby. ... All of this while there was a wheelbarrow full of putrid meat within 15 steps of him."

Charleston Museum Collections

"BLACK VULTURE OR CARRION CROW"
Black Vulture, *Coragyps atratus* (Bechstein)
Plate 106, *The Birds of America*, by John James Audubon

"Charleston, Savannah ... and other cities are amply provided with these birds, which may be seen flying or walking about the streets the whole day in groups.

" ... The Carrion Crows of Charleston resort at night to a swampy wood across the Ashley river, about two miles from the city. I visited this roosting place ... with my friend **JOHN BACHMAN**. ... When nearly under the trees on which the birds were roosted, we found the ground destitute of vegetation, and covered with odure and feathers. ... The stench was horrible. The trees were completely covered with birds ... the number of Vultures we estimated at several thousands."

AUDUBON, 1834, *Ornithological Biography***, Vol. II**

Private Collection

PROTHONOTARY WARBLER
Protonotaria citrea (Boddaert)

Plate 3, *The Birds of America*, by John James Audubon

"... Lakes, creeks and lagoons, overshadowed by large trees ... are favorite places of resort for this species. ... It often perches upon the rank grasses and water plants in quest of minute molluscous animals ... which, together with small land snails, I have found in its stomach."

AUDUBON, 1831, *Ornithological Biography*, Vol. 1

"DR. BACHMAN informs me that he has watched this species for hours at a time, when on the borders of streams, and observed it to seize insects on wing by gliding through the air after them, but never heard it click its bill, as is usual with Flycatchers. It breeds in South Carolina, and he saw a pair with four young ones near Charleston on the 1st of June 1836."

AUDUBON, 1839, *Ornithological Biography*, Vol. V

Private Collection

"SALT-WATER MARSH HEN"
Clapper Rail, *Rallus longirostris* **Boddaert**

Plate 204, *The Birds of America*, by John James Audubon

"About Charleston, in South Carolina, the shooting of Marsh Hens takes place from September to February, a few days in each month during the spring tides. ... There is no lack of shooting grounds, for every creek of salt-water swarms with Marsh Hens. ... As the boat moves swiftly toward them ... shot after shot flies in rapid succession; dead and dying lie all around in the water.

"... In the Carolinas there are some most expert marksmen. ... One of them I have seen shoot fifty Marsh Hens at fifty successive shots. ... On speaking once to a friend of the cruelty of destroying so many of these birds he answered me as follows: 'It gives variety to life, it is good exercise, and in all cases affords a capital dinner, besides the pleasure I feel when sending a mess of Marsh Hens to a friend such as you.'"

AUDUBON, 1835, *Ornithological Biography,* Vol. III

Private Collection

"THE RICE BIRD"
Bobolink, *Dolichonyx oryzivorus* (Linnaeus)

Plate 54, *The Birds of America*, by John James Audubon

"As they pass along the sea shores, and follow the muddy edges of the rivers, covered at that season with full grown reeds ... with ... ripe seeds, they alight amongst them in countless multitudes, and afford abundant practice to every gunner.

"... Millions of these birds are destroyed, and yet ... they ... reach the rice plantations of the Carolinas in such astonishing numbers, that no one could conceive their flocks have been already thinned. Their flesh is extremely tender and juicy."

AUDUBON, 1831, *Ornithological Biography*, Vol. I

Private Collection

AMERICAN WHITE PELICAN
Pelecanus erythrorhynchos Gmelin

Plate 311, *The Birds of America*, by John James Audubon

"My friend **JOHN BACHMAN**, in a note to me, says that 'this bird is now more rare on our coast than it was thirty years ago; for I have heard it stated that it formerly bred on the sand banks of our Bird Islands. I saw a flock on the Bird Banks off Bull's Island, on the 1st day of July 1814, when I procured two full-plumaged old birds, and was under the impression that they had laid eggs on one of those banks, but the latter had ... been overflowed by a spring tide.'"

AUDUBON, 1838, *Ornithological Biography*, Vol. IV

There are no authenticated records of the White Pelican nesting in South Carolina.

Private Collection

"LOUISIANA HERON"
Tricolored Heron, *Egretta tricolor* (Muller)

Watercolor on paper by Maria Martin, c. 1832

Copied from Audubon's original watercolor for Plate 217 of *The Birds of America,* this painting probably was done soon after Audubon's return to Charleston from Florida in May 1832. This talented sister-in-law of John Bachman was given instruction in the painting of birds by Audubon, and his style is clearly seen in this work.

Charleston Museum Collections

"LOUISIANA HERON"
Tricolored Heron, *Egretta tricolor* (Muller)

Plate 217, *The Birds of America*, by John James Audubon

"Delicate in form, beautiful in plumage, and graceful in its movements, I never see this interesting Heron, without calling it the Lady of the Waters. ... In the beginning of spring, it is found abundantly in the Carolinas. ... I have found them, breeding in company with the Green Heron and the Night Heron, within a few miles of Charleston.

AUDUBON, 1835, *Ornithological Biography,* Vol. III

Private Collection

"WOOD IBIS"
Wood Stork, *Mycteria americana* Linnaeus

Plate 216, *The Birds of America*, by John James Audubon

"The Wood ibis is said to breed about 25 miles from this place. The bird is certainly found at one place in this country in considerable numbers."

BACHMAN TO AUDUBON, 1 April 1833

"In the spring months, when these birds collect in large flocks, before they return to their breeding places, I have seen thousands together, passing over the woods in a line more than a mile in extent. ..."
AUDUBON, 1835, *Ornithological Biography*, Vol. III

Although rumored to breed in South Carolina for many years since Audubon's time, nests or eggs of this species were not discovered until 1981.

Now an endangered species

Private Collection

LONG-BILLED CURLEW
Numenius americanus Bechstein

Castle Pinckney at left and City of Charleston in background

Plate 231, *The Birds of America*, by John James Audubon

"The Long-billed Curlew ... is well known by the inhabitants of Charleston ... and my friend **JOHN BACHMAN** has been at their breeding grounds.

"... The Long-billed Curlew spends the day in the sea-marshes, from which it returns at the approach of night, to the sandy beaches of the sea-shores, where it rests until dawn. ... The number of birds that collect in the place selected for their nightly retreat, sometimes amounts to several thousand.

AUDUBON, 1835, *Ornithological Biography,* Vol. III

SEE PLATE 15, Page 147

Private Collection

"SNOWY HERON, OR WHITE EGRET"
Snowy Egret, *Egretta thula* (Molina)

South Carolina rice plantation in background

Plate 242, *The Birds of America*, by John James Audubon

"While I was at Charleston, in March of 1831, few had arrived from the Floridas by the 18th of that month, but on the 25th thousands were seen in the marshes and rice fields, all in full plumage. ... The Snowy Heron, while in the Carolinas, in the month of April, resorts to the borders of the salt-water marshes, and feeds principally on shrimps."

AUDUBON, 1835, *Ornithological Biography*, Vol. III

SEE PLATE 11, Page 143

Private Collection

SNOWY EGRET
Egretta thula (Molina)

Watercolor on paper by Maria Martin

Inscribed on back: "March 26, 1832 — Copied from Mr. Audubon's picture"

The picture to which Miss Martin refers was Audubon's original watercolor painting of the Snowy Egret (Plate 242, *The Birds of America*) which he completed at the Bachman home in 1832.

Private Collection

"SCHWARTZIA"

Watercolor on paper by Maria Martin, c. 1830

This delicately-executed plant study is currently identified only by the name "Schwartzia" in the upper right corner. Not a local plant, it is in all likelihood an exotic or cultivated form that may have been growing in John Bachman's garden.

Private Collection

MARIA MARTIN BACHMAN
1796 — 1863

Daguerreotype, c. 1850

Born in Charleston on 3 July 1796, Maria Martin was the youngest of four daughters of John Jacob and Rebecca Martin. Little is known of her early life, but her articulate letters and her literary and artistic interests indicate that she received as good an education as was offered young ladies of the early 19th century. When her sister, Harriet, married John Bachman in January 1816, Maria and her mother became a part of the new household.

Her talents as a watercolorist were noticed by John James Audubon during his first visit with the Bachmans in 1831, and she subsequently supplied many paintings of plants that were used as backgrounds for Audubon's birds in *The Birds of America*. In doing so, she became the only well-known South Carolina female artist of the 19th century.

After her sister Harriet's death in 1846, Maria married the Reverend John Bachman on 28 December 1848. She died at Columbia, S.C., on 27 December 1863.

Photo in Charleston Museum Collections

RETICULE

Made and decorated by Maria Martin

Talented ladies of the first half of the 19th century often found recreation in making their own handbags and decorating them with hand-painted motifs.

Charleston Museum Collections

BLACK RACER
Coluber constrictor Linnaeus

Illustration by Maria Martin

Plate II, Vol. 3, *North American Herpetology*, by John E. Holbrook, 1842

In addition to her plants for *The Birds of America*, Maria Martin also contributed the illustration of the Black Racer for Holbrook's monumental work on the reptiles and amphibians of North America. A prominent member of the Charleston scientific community, Holbrook produced the first comprehensive treatment of American herpetology.

Charleston Museum Collections

BUTTERFLY STUDIES

Watercolor by Maria Martin, 1833

Figure at lower right, apparently *Oenomaus ortygnus*, is seen at lower left in Plate 198 of *The Birds of America*, by John James Audubon.

"BROWN HEADED WORM EATING WARBLER"
Swainson's Warbler, *Limnothlypis swainsonii* (Audubon)

Plate 198, *The Birds of America*, by John James Audubon

"The bird represented in the plate before you was discovered by my friend **JOHN BACHMAN,** near Charleston in South Carolina. ... My southern friend found the first specimen of this bird, near the banks of the Edisto River. ... The Azalea and Butterflies accompanying the figure of this species were drawn by my friend's sister, **Miss MARTIN,** to whom I again offer my sincere thanks."

AUDUBON, 1834, *Ornithological Biography,* **Vol. II**

Named for the English ornithologist William Swainson, who lent assistance to Audubon.

Private Collection

WHITE PEACOCK BUTTERFLY
Anartia jatrophae guantanamo

Watercolor by Maria Martin, 1833

Original studies for figures in Plate 355, *The Birds of America*, by John James Audubon.

SEE PLATE 10, Page 142

Charleston Museum Collections

"MACGILLIVRAY'S FINCH"
MacGillivray's Seaside Sparrow, *Ammodramus maritimus* (Wilson)

Plate 355, *The Birds of America*, by John James Audubon

"Another species of Finch ... which ... is found abundantly in the salt marshes of the Carolinas, has been discovered by my ... friend ... **JOHN BACHMAN** of Charleston, who has presented me with a dozen specimens of it. ... The figures of this newly discovered species ... were drawn at Charleston by my son **JOHN WOOD-HOUSE**. ..."

AUDUBON, 1834, *Ornithological Biography,* Vol. III

The figures of the White Peacock Butterfly, *Anartia jatrophae guantanamo,* are the work of Maria Martin.

Private Collection

"I need not inform you that Mr. Audubon was a general favorite in our city. ... He taught my sister Maria to draw birds; and she has now such a passion for it, that whilst I am writing, she is drawing a Bittern, put up for her at daylight by Mr. Audubon."

JOHN BACHMAN TO LUCY AUDUBON, 15 November 1831

"Today I perceive in the papers that my old friend Audubon has been heard of at some island far north. I hope you have also received some more particular intelligence from him, and above all, I hope ere long to take him once more by the hand. ... I have been working among insects and have had my artist painting butterflies all summer, which I fear she does not relish particularly well."

JOHN BACHMAN TO LUCY AUDUBON, 4 September 1833

"Here under the roof of our good Friend John Bachman we are all comfortable & employed in writing, drawing, music, reading & conversing from the moment we raise in the Morning until we retire to rest."

JOHN JAMES AUDUBON TO VICTOR AUDUBON, 4 November 1833

"Charleston, S.C., Nov. 17, 1836. We arrived here last evening after an irksome and fatiguing journey, and seemingly very slowly performed, in my anxiety to reach a resting place, where friendship and love would combine to render our time happy, and the prosecution of our labor pleasant. We were hungry, thirsty, and dusty as ... could be; but we found our dear friends all well, tears of joy ran from their eyes, and we embraced the whole of them as if born from one mother. John Bachman was absent from home, but returned at nine from his presidential chair at the Philosophical Society."

JOHN JAMES AUDUBON, *Journal*

PIANO STOOL

Given to Maria Martin by John James Audubon, c. 1838

Charleston Museum Collections

A Vanishing Era

IVORY-BILLED WOODPECKER
Campephilus principalis (Linnaeus)

Nearing extinction

"Its notes are clear, loud, and yet rather plaintive. They are heard at a considerable distance, perhaps half a mile, and resemble the false high note of a clarionet. They are ... heard so frequently as to induce me to say that the bird spends few minutes of the day without uttering them, and this circumstance leads to its destruction, which is aimed at, not because (as is supposed by some) this species is a destroyer of trees, but more because it is a beautiful bird, and its rich scalp attached to the upper mandible forms an ornament for the war-dress of most of our Indians, or for the shot-pouch of our squatters and hunters, by all of whom the bird is shot merely for that purpose.

"... I have frequently remarked, that on a steam-boat's reaching what we call a *wooding place,* the *strangers* were very apt to pay a quarter of a dollar for two or three heads of this Woodpecker. I have seen entire belts of Indian chiefs closely ornamented with the tufts and bills of this species, and have observed that a great value is frequently put upon them."

AUDUBON, 1831, *Ornithological Biography*, Vol. 1

Charleston Museum Collections No. 30.147.512
Wacissa River, Florida; Arthur T. Wayne, 30 March 1907. Adult male.

IVORY-BILLED WOODPECKER
Campephilus principalis (Linnaeus)

Plate 66, *The Birds of America,* by John James Audubon

"I wish it were in my power to present to your mind's eye the favourite resort of the Ivory-billed Woodpecker. Would that I could describe the extent of those deep morasses, overshadowed by millions of gigantic dark cypresses ... extending for miles. ... Would that I could represent to you the dangerous nature of the ground, its oozy, spongy, and miry disposition, although covered with a beautiful but treacherous carpeting ... of the richest mosses, flags, and water-lilies. ..."

AUDUBON, 1831, *Ornithological Biography,* Vol. I

Courtesy of the Robert Scott Small Library at The College of Charleston

89

"THE CAROLINA PARROT"
Carolina Parakeet, *Conuropsis carolinensis* (Linnaeus)

Plate 26, *The Birds of America,* by John James Audubon

"These birds are represented feeding on the plant commonly named the *Cockle-bur* ... on the seeds of which the Parrot feeds. ... The Parrot ... eats or destroys almost every kind of fruit indiscrimately, and on this account is always an unwelcome visitor to the planter.

"The Parakeets are destroyed in great numbers ... whilst busily engaged in tearing off the fruits. ... I have seen several hundred destroyed ... in the course of a few hours, and have procured ... a choice of good specimens for drawing the figures ... in the plate now under your consideration."

AUDUBON, 1831, *Ornithological Biography*, Vol. I

EXTINCT. The last known Carolina Parakeet died in the Cincinnati Zoo in 1914.

SEE PLATE 9, Page 141   *Private Collection*

CAROLINA PARAKEET
Conuropsis carolinensis (Linnaeus)

"Our Parakeets are very rapidly diminishing in number; and in some districts, where twenty-five years ago, they were plentiful, scarcely any are now to be seen."

AUDUBON, 1831, *Ornithological Biography*, Vol. 1

Charleston Museum Collections, No. 30.147.414
Lake Locke, Florida, Arthur T. Wayne, 5 November 1892

PASSENGER PIGEON
Ectopistes migratorius (Linnaeus)

Plate 62, *The Birds of America,* by John James Audubon

"The multitudes of Wild Pigeons in our woods are astonishing. ... On such occasions, when the woods are filled with these pigeons, they are killed in immense numbers. Persons unacquainted with these birds might naturally conclude that such dreadful havock would soon put an end to the species. But I have satisfied myself ... that nothing but the gradual diminuation of our forests can accomplish their decrease. ..."

AUDUBON, 1831, *Ornithological Biography*, Vol. I

EXTINCT. The last known Passenger Pigeon died in the Cincinnati Zoo in 1914

Private Collection

PASSENGER PIGEON
Ectopistes migratorius (Linnaeus)

Extinct

"As the sun begins to sink beneath the horizon, they depart *en masse* for the roosting place. ... One of these I repeatedly visited. ... Few pigeons were then to be seen, but a great number of persons, with horses and wagons, guns and ammunition, had already established encampments on the borders. ... Everything proved to me that the number of birds resorting to this part of the forest must be immense beyond conception. ... Suddenly there burst forth a general cry of 'Here they come!' ... As the birds arrived and passed over me, I felt a current of air that surprised me. ... The Pigeons, arriving by thousands, alighted everywhere, one above another, until solid masses as large as hogsheads were formed on the branches all round. Here and there the perches gave way under the weight with a crash, and falling to the ground, destroyed hundreds of the birds beneath. ... It was a scene of uproar and confusion. ... Even the reports of the guns were seldom heard, and I was made aware of the firing only by seeing the shooters reloading.

"... Towards the approach of day ... the authors of all this devastation began their entry among the dead, the dying and the mangled. The pigeons were picked up and piled in heaps, until each had as many as he could dispose of, when the hogs were let loose to feed on the remainder."

AUDUBON, 1831, *Ornithological Biography*, Vol. I

Charleston Museum Collections, No. 52.117.1155
Redwing, Minnesota, H.W. Howard, 10 May 1886. Adult male

ESKIMO CURLEW
Numenius borealis (Forster)

Charleston Museum Collections, No. 30.147.229
Davenport, Iowa, M.A. Frazier, 3 May 1901. Adult female

PLATE CC

ESKIMO CURLEW
Numenius borealis (Forster)

Plate 208, *The Birds of America*, by John James Audubon

"On one occasion only have I ever had a glimpse of it. I was in company with my learned and generous friend **JOHN BACHMAN** of Charleston, on one of the islands on the coast of South Carolina. ... It was at the dawn of a fine day, when a dense flock of the northern Curlews passed to the southward, near enough to enable us to ascertain the species, but so swiftly, that in a few minutes they were quite out of sight."

AUDUBON, 1835, *Ornithological Biography*, Vol. III

Nearing extinction in North America

Courtesy of the Charleston Library Society

"John too may want a little recreation & his big gun can only talk to the purpose at Goose Creek. I have had but one chance of going into the country & that was last week for two days a part of which were taken up in the journey — Desel killed a deer — & I tumbled over three fine fellows — one of which however was lost in the river — a famous buck of my shooting is now sitting up in the Museum."

BACHMAN TO AUDUBON, 26 January 1840

ROSE HILL PLANTATION

Oil on canvas. Artist unknown, c. 1825

Located along the banks of the Combahee River in Colleton County, "Rose Hill" was typical of the many plantations that dotted the South Carolina Lowcountry in the days of Audubon and Bachman.

During Audubon's visits to Charleston he and John Bachman were frequent guests at "Liberty Hall" plantation near Charleston, the home of Bachman's good friend, Doctor Desel. There they hunted deer and enjoyed the relaxing atmosphere of plantation life.

But, like the Passenger Pigeons, Carolina Parakeets and Ivory-billed Woodpeckers that flew over them, these mighty holdings were part of an era that was vanishing almost without notice.

SEE PLATE 16, Page 148   *Charleston Museum Collections*

Into The Sunset

AUDUBON AND BACHMAN AND *THE QUADRUPEDS OF NORTH AMERICA*

As work on *The Birds of America* neared completion, Audubon began to look toward a similar work on the North American mammals, or "quadrupeds," as they also were called at that time. Most of them were not well known and few had been illustrated in color.

In his letter of 13 September 1839, John Bachman cautioned Audubon that "The animals ... have never been carefully described, and you will find difficulties at every step. The Books cannot aid you much. Long journeys will have to be undertaken. ... I wish I had you here for only two days. I think I have studied the subject more than you have."

Recognizing his old friend's superior knowledge of mammals, Audubon enlisted Bachman's aid in writing the text for the proposed work.

"About this partnership in the Quadrupeds we will talk more about when we meet. ... Don't flatter yourself that this Book is childs play — the birds are a mere trifle compared to this. I have been at it all my life ... we all have much to learn in this matter."

BACHMAN TO AUDUBON, 13 January 1840

RED SQUIRRELS
"Sciurus hudsonius," Tamiasciurus hudsonicus (Erxleben)

Watercolor on paper by John James Audubon, 9 November 1839

Painted soon after his return to America after completing the final volume of the *Ornithological Biography*, these figures are the basis for Plate 14 of *The Viviparous Quadrupeds of North America.*

After John Bachman had agreed to collaborate on the text, Audubon threw himself into the task of painting North American mammals with all the enthusiasm that he had lavished on the birds. "I am now as anxious about the publication of the Quadrupeds as I ever was in the procuring of our Birds," he wrote to young Spencer Baird of Carlisle, Pennsylvania, on 29 July 1841.

SEE PLATE 3, Page 135

Private Collection

THE

VIVIPAROUS QUADRUPEDS

OF

NORTH AMERICA.

BY

JOHN JAMES AUDUBON, F.R.S., &c., &c.

AND

THE REV. JOHN BACHMAN, D.D., LL.D., &c. &c.

VOL. II.

NEW-YORK:
PUBLISHED BY V. G. AUDUBON.
M DCCC LI.

TITLE PAGE OF TEXT

The Viviparous Quadrupeds of North America, Volume II, 1851

The first edition, entitled *The Viviparous Quadrupeds of North America,* consisted of two unbound volumes of 150 colored lithographs in imperial folio size published in 1845 and 1846. The text, written by John Bachman, appeared in three volumes published between 1846 and 1854.

A second edition, entitled *The Quadrupeds of North America*, was published in royal-octavo size in 1854 and included both the plates and the text.

A hard, strenuous undertaking that took its toll on both Audubon and Bachman, *The Quadrupeds of North America* was acclaimed at home and abroad as the finest work that had yet been published on the mammals of North America.

Private Collection

WOODCHUCKS
Marmota monax **Blumenbach**

Watercolor on paper by John James Audubon, New York, 11 July 1841

Original painting for Plate 2 of *The Viviparous Quadrupeds of North America.*

This marvelous study is further evidence of Audubon's genius with his brushes. After years of painting feathers he showed equal facility in depicting fur and here has captured the rich, lustrous pelage of his subjects with admirable skill.

SEE PLATE 4, Page 136

WOODCHUCKS
Marmota monax Blumenbach

Plate 2, *The Viviparous Quadrupeds of North America,* by John James Audubon

Printers proof sheet retouched by John James Audubon.

The rust color of the fore and hind limbs and the fine white hairs are corrections added in watercolor by Audubon.

Penciled notations by Audubon are as follows:

Title at center:
Arctomys monax, Gmel.

Lower left corner:
Drawn from Life
By J.J. Audubon

Note that the positions of the two smaller figures in the original have been reversed in the proof.

Presented to The Charleston Museum in 1911
by Florence Audubon, granddaughter of John James Audubon

103

"MARYLAND MARMOT, GROUND HOG, WOODCHUCK"
Ground Hog, Woodchuck, *Marmota monax* Blumenbach

Plate 2, *The Viviparous Quadrupeds of North America,* by Audubon and Bachman, Vol. 1

Published print, Imperial Folio Edition

"We have found the Wood-Chuck in every State of the Union north-east of South Carolina, and throughout the Canadas, Nova Scotia, and New Brunswick. ... It is not found in the maritime districts either of North or South Carolina, but exists very sparingly in the mountainous regions of those States."
AUDUBON AND BACHMAN, 1846, *The Quadrupeds of North America,* Vol. I

Courtesy of The Middleton Place Foundation

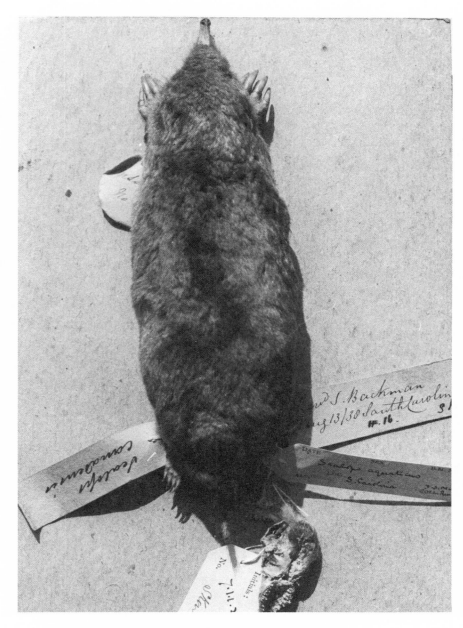

EASTERN MOLE
Scalopus aquaticus howelli Jackson

South Carolina specimen collected and prepared by John Bachman

In his preparation of the text for *The Viviparous Quadrupeds of North America*, Bachman drew upon Audubon's notes and his own experience in mammalian descriptive taxonomy. By 1838 he had published three papers on North American mammals, one of which he read before the renowned Zoological Society of London in August 1838. The specimen above is one of nine mammal skins that Bachman presented to the Society on that occasion. All have been excellently preserved in the mammal collection of the British Museum (Natural History).

BM (NH) No. 7.1.1.21
Photo by Albert E. Sanders, courtesy of the Mammal Section,
British Museum (Natural History)

COMMON AMERICAN WILDCAT
Lynx rufus Kerr

Plate 1, *The Viviparous Quadrupeds of North America*, by Audubon and Bachman

"An individual that was kept alive at Charleston, ... showed its affinity to the domestic cat, by purring and mewing at times loud enough to be heard at some distance. At the former place its cry was several times mistaken for that of the common house-cat. In the woods, during the winter season, its loud catterwauling can be heard at the distance of a mile.

"... We once made an attempt at domesticating one of the young of this species, which we obtained when only two weeks old. It was a most spiteful, growling, snappish little wretch, and showed no disposition to improve its habits and manners. ... It, one night, escaped into our library, where it made sad work among the books ... and left the marks of its teeth on the mutilated window sashes."
AUDUBON AND BACHMAN, 1846, *The Viviparous Quadrupeds of North America*, Vol. I

Private Collection

"CAROLINA GREY SQUIRREL"
Gray Squirrel, *Sciurus carolinensis* Ord

Plate 7, *The Viviparous Quadrupeds of North America*, by Audubon and Bachman

"... Its usual haunts are low swampy places or trees overhanging streams or growing near the margin of some river. In deep cypress swamps covered in many places with several feet of water during the whole year, it takes up its constant residence. ... On the large Tupelo trees (*Nyssa aquatica*), which are found in the swamps, many nests of this species, composed principally of Spanish moss and leaves, are everywhere to be seen."
AUDUBON AND BACHMAN, 1846, *The Viviparous Quadrupeds of North America*, Vol. I

Private Collection

LEPUS PALUSTRIS, BACHMAN.
MARSH HARE.

"MARSH HARE"
Marsh Rabbit, *Sylvilgagus palustris* (Bachman)

Plate 18, *The Viviparous Quadrupeds of North America*, by Audubon and Bachman

First described by John Bachman as *Lepus palustris* in the Journal of the Academy of Natural Sciences of Philadelphia in 1837.

"The Marsh-Hare chiefly confines itself to the maritime districts of the southern States, and is generally found in low marshy grounds that are sometimes partially inundated, near rivers subject to freshets that ... overflow their banks, or near the large ponds called in Carolina 'reserves,' which are ... made to retain the water ... to flood the rice-fields at the proper season."
AUDUBON AND BACHMAN, 1846, *The Viviparous Quadrupeds of North America*, Vol. I

Private Collection

"GREY FOX"
Gray Fox, *Urocyon cinereoargenteus* Baird

Plate 21, *The Viviparous Quadrupeds of North America*, by Audubon and Bachman

"On a cold, drizzly, sleety, rainy day, while traveling in Carolina, we observed a Gray Fox in a field of broom-grass, coursing against the wind, and hunting in the manner of the pointer dog. We stopped to witness his manoeuvres: suddenly he stood still and squatted low on his haunches; a moment after he proceeded on once more, but with slow and cautious steps; at times his nose was raised high in the air, moving about from side to side. At length he seemed to be sure of his game ... then made a sudden pounce upon his prey ... and ... immediately passed out of the field with an unfortunate partridge in his mouth.

"... Shortly after the railroad from Charleston to Hamburgh, South Carolina, had been constructed, the rails for a portion of the distance having been laid upon timbers at a considerable height from the ground, supported by strong posts, we observed a Fox which was hard pressed by a pack of hounds, mounting the rails ... and he thus crossed a deep cypress swamp ... and made his escape on the opposite side."
AUDUBON AND BACHMAN, 1846, *The Viviparous Quadrupeds of North America*, **Vol. I**

Private Collection

COTTON RAT
Sigmodon hispidus Say and Ord

Plate 30, *The Viviparous Quadrupeds of North America*, by Audubon and Bachman

"This is the most common wood-rat existing in the Southern States. ... It is ... a resident ... of hedges, ditches and deserted old fields.

"... The Cotton-Rat is fond of burrowing in the old banks of abandoned rice-fields. In such situations we have, during freshets, observed that it could both swim and dive.

"... This species supplies a considerable number of animals ... with food. ... We were invited some years since to examine the nest of the American barn-owl ... in the loft of a sugar refinery in Charleston. There were several young of different sizes, and we ascertained that the only food on which they were fed was this Rat, to obtain which the old birds must have gone several miles."

AUDUBON AND BACHMAN, 1846, *The Viviparous Quadrupeds of North America*, Vol. I

Private Collection

SOREX CAROLINENSIS, BACH.
CAROLINA SHREW.
MALES & FEMALE

"CAROLINA SHREW"
Short-tailed Shrew, *Blarina carolinensis* (Bachman)

Plate 75, *The Viviparous Quadrupeds of North America*, by Audubon and Bachman

"This quadruped is found in various localities, both in the upper and maritime districts of South Carolina. We recently received specimens from our friend **Dr. BARRETT**, of Abbeville District; and we have been informed by **Dr. PICKERING** ... that it had been observed as far north as Philadelphia."
AUDUBON AND BACHMAN, 1851, *The Viviparous Quadrupeds of North America* Vol. II

Courtesy of Edward Kenney, Audubon Prints and Books, Washington, D.C.

One More Time

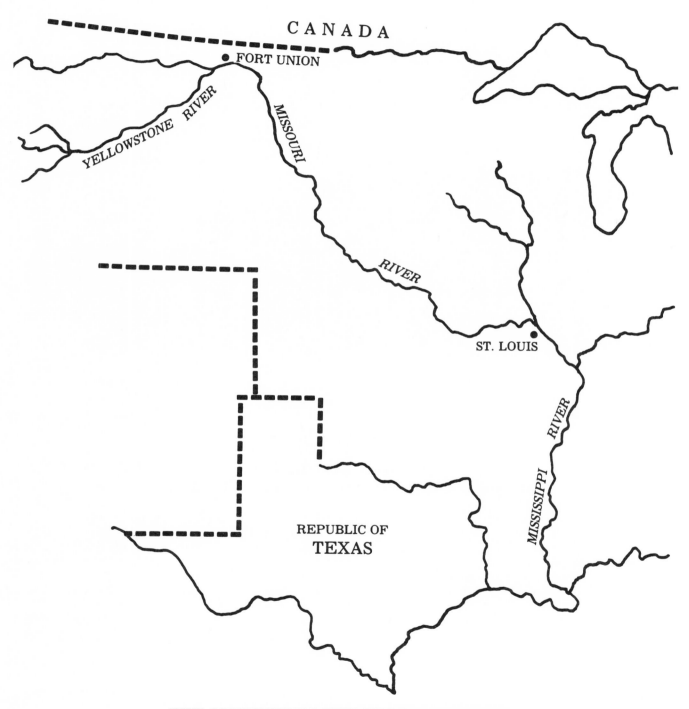

THE JOURNEY TO THE UPPER MISSOURI
April — November 1843

AMERICAN BISON
Bison bison Linnaeus

Plate 57, *The Viviparous Quadrupeds of North America*, by Audubon and Bachman

By 1842 it became clear to Audubon and Bachman that they badly needed specimens of the Western mammals. Audubon had dreamed of a trip to the West for many years, and he now determined to make the journey. At age 58, he knew that it would be his last major excursion into the wilderness.

Accompanied by a party of four that included Isaac Sprague, an artist, and Audubon's old friend Edward Harris, he left St. Louis aboard the steamer *Omega* on 25 April 1843 and began the ascent of the Missouri River. Forty-eight days later, on 12 June, the party reached Fort Union at the mouth of the Yellowstone River. They remained there for two months and hunted among the vast herds of bison that became symbolic of the American West.

Audubon's keen eye soon detected ominous signs in the relentless hunting of the Bison, and on 5 August he made the following entry in his journal:

"One can hardly conceive how it happens, notwithstanding ... the immense numbers that are murdered almost daily on these boundless wastes ... so many are yet to be found. ... But this cannot last; even now there is a perceptible difference in the size of the herds, and before many years the Buffalo, like the Great Auk, will have disappeared; surely this should not be permitted."

On 16 August the party left Fort Union on their return homeward, and on 6 November 1843 a weary Audubon rejoined his family in New York. The Great Adventure was over.

Private Collection

POWDER HORN WITH SCRIMSHAW
Carving by John James Audubon

A souvenir of his trip up the Missouri River in 1843, this bison horn is decorated with Western scenes carved by Audubon.

Private Collection

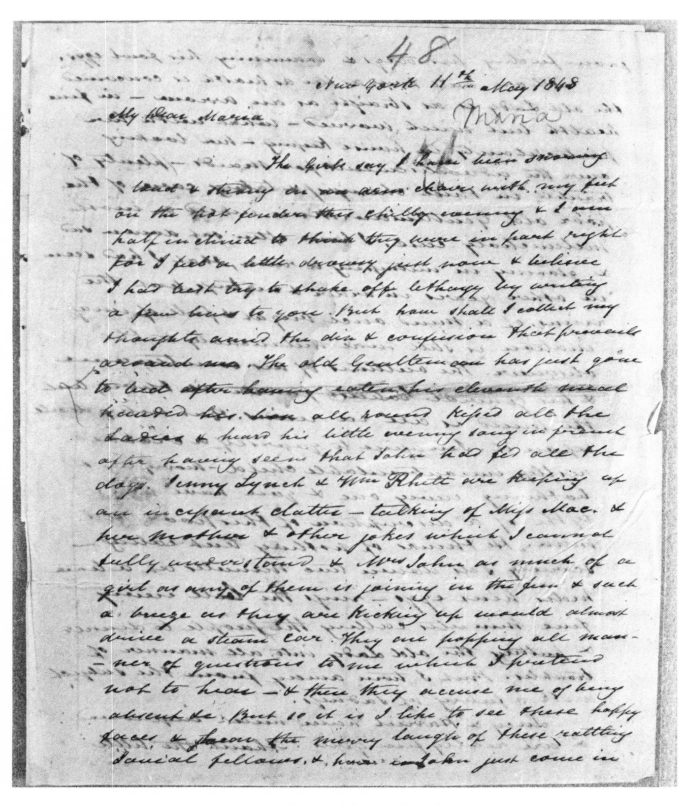

New York 11th May 1848

My Dear Maria —

Mina

The whole day I have been snowing and hurry on an arm chair with my feet on the hot fender this chilly evening & I am half inclined to think they were in part right for I feel a little drowsy just now & believe I had best try to shake off lethargy by writing a few lines to you. But how shall I collect my thoughts amid the din & confusion that prevails around me. The old Gentleman has just gone to bed after having eaten his eleventh meal hearded his lion all round Kissed all the Ladies & heard his little evening song in friend after having seen that John had fed all the dogs. Jenny Lynch & Wm Rhett are Keeping up an incessant clatter — talking of Miss Mac. & her mother & other jokes which I cannot fully understand & Mrs John as much of a girl as any of them is joining in the fun & such a breeze as they are Kicking up would almost drive a steam car They are popping all manner of questions to me which I pretend not to hear — & then they accuse me of being absent &c. But so it is I like to see these happy faces & hear the merry laugh of these rattling Sensiol fellows. & how in John just come in

JOHN BACHMAN TO MARIA MARTIN, 11 May 1848

Charleston Museum Collections

"A MOST MELANCHOLY CASE"
John James Audubon
Daguerreotype, 1850

In 1846 Audubon's eyesight began to fail, and he could paint no more. Gradually, his mind also began to slip away. His son, John Woodhouse Audubon, assumed the task of completing the paintings for the *Quadrupeds*.

In May 1848, John Bachman visited the Audubons at their beloved "Minnie's Land," overlooking the Hudson River on the outskirts of New York City. Writing to Maria Martin on 11 May 1848, he expressed his distress at his old friend's condition:

"The old Gentleman has just gone to bed after having ... kissed all the Ladies & heard his little song in French. ... His is indeed a most melancholy case. ... The outlines of his countenance & his general robust appearance are there, but the mind is all in ruins. ... I turn away from the subject with a feeling of sadness."

"COMMON OR VIRGINIAN DEER"
White-Tailed Deer, *Odocoileus virginianus* (Zimmermann)

Plate 136, *The Viviparous Quadrupeds of North America*, by Audubon and Bachman

John Woodhouse Audubon had now assumed the task of completing the illustrations for *Quadrupeds*, and this figure is one of his best works.

"A very large and healthy doe often produces three, and we were present at Goose Creek when an immense one, killed by **J.W. AUDUBON**, was ascertained, on being opened, to contain four large and well formed fawns."

AUDUBON AND BACHMAN, 1851, *The Viviparous Quadrupeds of North America*, Vol. II

Private Collection

"CANADA OTTER"
River Otter, *Lutra canadensis* Sabine

Plate 122, *The Viviparous Quadrupeds of North America*, by Audubon and Bachman

"The habit of the Otter of sliding down from elevated places to the borders of streams, is not confined to cold countries ... but is pursued in the Southern States. ... Along the reserve-dams of the rice-fields of Carolina and Georgia, these slides are very common.

"... About twenty-five years ago we went early one autumnal morning to study the habits of the Otter at Gordon and Spring's Ferry, on the Cooper River, six miles above Charleston, where they were represented as being quite abundant. They came down with the receding tide in groups or families of five or six together. In the space of two hours we counted forty-six. They soon separated, ascended the different creeks in the salt marshes, and engaged in capturing mullets."
AUDUBON AND BACHMAN, 1851, *The Viviparous Quadrupeds of North America*, Vol. II

Private Collection

My Dear Friend

I wrote to you before I got your excellent and
affectionate letter, to beg you would buy and come to stay
some time with us for the benefit of your health as well
as to give us pleasure, in my letter which must have
passed yours on the way, I reminded you that as the
family now, consisted of only four you might all
come together and a few months in this latitude would
be of service to you all Victor says he wishes to write &
I repeat my request to you hoping you will all act
upon it, the visit to me will be a great pleasure in which
I am sure all will participate in the house . We had at
dinner to day Mr Dite Artist who mentioned the death of
Mrs Doctor Wilson, of which we had never heard, can it be
true? You will find some changes in the outward as
well as indoor circumstances around us, and I fear there
is no greater inducement for Jane or Catty than the bathing
which is still good — I have been planting various favou
=rite shrubs and creepers over the resting place of my poor
old friend, who seems as quiet as solemn in his cell as the
mind can concieve, and all but the remembrance of him
and his goodness to me is gone forever. I am always glad
to hear of you all being well and happy, Lucy and Harriet
desire their love to you, and to Grand Papa and all round, in
which I heartily join . Mr & Mrs Hall and some of the children

LUCY AUDUBON TO MARIA MARTIN BACHMAN, 31 March 1851

Charleston Museum Collections

"ALL BUT THE REMEMBRANCE OF HIM IS GONE FOREVER"
Lucy Audubon
Daguerreotype, 1854

"After a few days of increasing feebleness ... just as sunset was flooding the pure, snow-covered landscape with golden light, at five o'clock on Monday, January 27, 1851," John James Audubon passed away.
MARIA R. AUDUBON, *Audubon and his Journals,* **Vol. 1, p. 77**

"I have been planting various favourite shrubs and weepers over the resting place of my poor old friend, who seems as quiet ... in his cell as the mind can conceive, and all but the remembrance of him and his goodness to me is gone forever."

LUCY AUDUBON TO MARIA MARTIN BACHMAN, 31 March 1851

Photo courtesy of The New York Historical Society

Monuments

JOHN JAMES AUDUBON
Copy of life mask made by Robert Havell in 1830

Model for the bust of John James Audubon sculpted by Joy Buba for the National Audubon Society in 1955.

Often obscured by his fame as an artist, Audubon's contributions to science included the descriptions of 23 new birds and, in collaboration with John Bachman, of ten new mammals. In the *Ornithological Biography* he provided many valuable observations on the life histories of North American birds.

Private Collection

NEW BIRDS DESCRIBED BY JOHN JAMES AUDUBON

1. Black-footed Albatross   *Diomedea nigripes* Audubon
    Diomedea nigripes Audubon.   *Ornithological Biography* (1839), 5:327.

* 2. King Rail   *Rallus elegans* Audubon
    Rallus elegans Audubon.   *The Birds of America* (1834), 3: pl. 203;   *Ornith. Biogr.* (1835), 3:27.

3. American Black Oystercatcher   *Haematopus bachmani* Audubon
    Haematopus bachmani Audubon.   *Birds Amer.* (1838) (folio), 4: pl. 427, Fig. 1;   *Ornith. Biogr.* (1839), 5:245.

4. Western Gull   *Larus occidentalis* Audubon
    Larus occidentalis Audubon.   *Ornith. Biogr.* (1839), 5:320.

5. Trudeau's Tern, Snowy-crowned Tern   *Sterna trudeaui* Audubon
    Sterna trudeaui Audubon.   *Birds Amer.* (1838) (folio), 4: pl. 409, fig. 2;   *Ornith. Biogr.* (1839), 5:125.

6. Common Poorwill   *Phalaenoptilus nuttalli* Audubon
    Caprimulgus nuttalli Audubon   *Birds Amer.* (1844) (octavo ed.), 7:350, pl. 495.

7. Willow Flycatcher   *Empidonax traillii* (Audubon)
    Muscicapa traillii Audubon.   *Birds Amer.* (1828) (folio), 1: pl. 45;   *Ornith. Biogr.* (1831), 1:236.

* 8. Northern Rough-winged Swallow   *Stelgidopteryx serripennis* (Audubon)
    Hirundo serripennis Audubon.   *Ornith. Biogr.* (1838), 4:93.

9. Yellow-billed Magpie   *Pica nuttalli* (Audubon)
    Corvus nuttalli (sic) Audubon.   *Birds Amer.* (1837) (folio), 4: pl. 362, Fig. 1.

* 10. Carolina Chickadee   *Parus carolinensis* Audubon
    Parus carolinensis Audubon.   *Ornith. Biogr.* (1834), 2:341.

11 Bewick's Wren   *Thryomanes bewickii* (Audubon)
    Troglodytes bewickii Audubon.   *Birds Amer.* (1827) (folio), 1: pl. 18;   *Ornith. Biogr.* (1831), 1:96.

12. Townsend's Solitaire   *Myadestes townsendi* (Audubon)
    Ptilogony's (sic) *Townsendi* Audubon.   *Birds Amer.* (1838) (folio), 4: pl. 419, Fig. 2;   *Ornith. Biogr.* (1839), 5:206.

13. Sprague's Pipit   *Anthus spragueii* (Audubon)
    Alauda spragueii Audubon   *Birds Amer.* (1844) (octavo ed.), 7:334, pl. 486.

14. Bell's Vireo   *Vireo bellii* Audubon
    Vireo bellii Audubon   *Birds Amer.* (1844) (octavo ed.), 7:333, pl. 485.

* 15. Bachman's Warbler   *Vermivora bachmanii* (Audubon)
    Sylvia Bachmanii Audubon.   *Birds Amer.* (1833) (folio), 2: pl. 185;   *Ornith. Biogr.* (1834), 2:483.

* 16. Swainson's Warbler   *Limnothlypis swainsonii* (Audubon)
    Sylvia Swainsonii Audubon   *Birds Amer.* (1834) (folio), 2; pl. 198;   *Ornith. Biogr.* (1834), 2:563.

17. Green-tailed Towhee   *Pipilo chlorurus* (Audubon)
    Fringilla chlorura Audubon   *Ornith. Biogr.* (1839), 5:336.

18. Baird's Sparrow   *Ammodramus bairdii* (Audubon)
    Emberiza Bairdii Audubon.   *Birds Amer.* (1844) (octavo ed.), 7: 359, pl. 500.

19. Henslow's Sparrow   *Ammodramus henslowii* (Audubon)
    Emberiza Henslowii Audubon.   *Birds Amer.* (1829) (folio), 1: pl. 70;   *Ornith. Biogr.* (1831), 1:360.

20. Le Conte's Sparrow   *Ammodramus leconteii* (Audubon)
    Emberiza le conteii Audubon.   *Birds Amer.* (1844) (octavo ed.), 7:338, pl. 488.

21. Lincoln's Sparrow   *Melospiza lincolnii* (Audubon)
    Fringilla Lincolnii Audubon.   *Birds Amer.* (1834) (folio), 2; pl. 193.

22. Tricolored Blackbird   *Agelaius tricolor* (Audubon)
    Icterus tricolor Audubon.   *Birds Amer.* (1837) (folio), 4: pl. 388, fig. 1;   *Ornith. Biogr.* (1839), 5:1.

23. Western Meadowlark   *Sturnella neglecta* Audubon
    Sturnella neglecta Audubon.   *Birds Amer.* (1844) (octavo ed.), 7:339, pl. 489.

* Original (or "type") specimen from South Carolina.

"Possibly the only way that I shall ride to immortality will be on the back of a mole or a rat."
JOHN BACHMAN TO JOHN WOODHOUSE AUDUBON, 7 April 1833

JOHN BACHMAN

Plaster bust by unidentified artist, possibly from life mask by Clark Mills

An excellent likeness of a remarkable man, whose motto, "Nature, Truth, and no Humbug," reflected the honesty and integrity that made him one of the most respected men of his time.

Although often overshadowed by Audubon's fame, John Bachman was a highly capable naturalist who personally described twenty new kinds of North American mammals and added ten more forms in collaboration with John James Audubon.

Charleston Museum Collections

NEW MAMMALS DESCRIBED BY AUDUBON AND BACHMAN

* 1. Southeastern Shrew   *Sorex longirostris longirostris* Bachman
     1837. *Sorex longirostris* Bachman   *Journal of the Academy of Natural Sciences of Philadelphia*, Ser. 1, 7(2):370.

* 2. Short-tailed Shrew   *Blarina carolinensis* (Bachman)
     1837. *Sorex carolinensis* Bachman.   *J. Acad. Nat. Sci. Philadelphia*, 7(2):366.

3. Townsend's Mole   *Scapanus townsendii* (Bachman)
     1839. *Scalops Townsendii* Bachman.   *J. Acad. Nat. Sci. Philadelphia, 8:58.*

4. Broad-footed Mole   *Scapanus latimanus latimanus* (Bachman)
     1842. *Scalops latimanus* Bachman.   *Boston Journal of Natural History*, 4:34.

5. Hairy-tailed Mole   *Parascalops breweri* (Bachman)
     1842. *Scalops breweri* Bachman.   *Boston J. Nat. Hist.*, 4:32.

6. Nuttall's Cottontail   *Sylvilagus nuttallii nuttallii* (Bachman)
     1837. *Lepus nuttallii* Bachman.   *J. Acad. Nat. Sci. Philadelphia*, 7:345.

7. Swamp Rabbit   *Sylvilagus aquaticus aquaticus* (Bachman)
     1837. *Lepus aquaticus* Bachman.   *J. Acad. Nat. Sci. Philadelphia*, 7:319.

8. White-tailed Jack Rabbit   *Lepus townsendii townsendii* Bachman
     1839. *Lepus townsendii* Bachman.   *J. Acad. Nat. Sci. Philadelphia*, 8(Pt. 1):90, Pl. 2.

* 9. Marsh Rabbit   *Sylvilagus palustris palustris* (Bachman)
     1837. *Lepus palustris* Bachman.   *J. Acad. Nat. Sci. Philadelphia*, 7:194.

10. Black-tailed Jack Rabbit   *Lepus californicus richardsonii* Bachman
     1839. *Lepus richardsonii* Bachman.   *J. Acad. Nat. Sci. Philadelphia*, 8(Pt. 1):88.

11. Least Chipmunk   *Eutamias minimus minimus* (Bachman)
     1839. *Tamias minimus* Bachman.   *J. Acad. Nat. Sci. Philadelphia*, 8:71.

12. Yellow-bellied Marmot   *Marmota flaviventris flaviviventris*, (Audubon & Bachman)
     1841. *Arctomys flaviventer* Audubon & Bachman.   *Proceedings of the Academy of Natural Sciences of philadelphia*, 1:99.

13. Townsend's Ground Squirrel   *Spermophilus townsendii townsendii* Bachman
     1839. *Spermophilus townsendii* Bachman.   *J. Acad. Nat. Sci. Philadelphia*, 8:61.

14. Ring-tailed Ground Squirrel   *Spermophilus annulatus annulatus* Audubon & Bachman
     1842. *Spermophilus annulatus* Audubon & Bachman.   *J. Acad. Nat. Sci. Philadelphia*, 8:319.

15. Gray Squirrel   *Sciurus carolinensis fuliginosus* Bachman
     1839. *Sciurus fuliginosus* Bachman.   *Proceedings of the Zoological Society of London*, 1838:97.

16. Fox Squirrel   *Sciurus niger subauratus* Bachman
     1839 *Sciurus subauratus* Bachman.   *Proc. Zool. Soc. London*, 1838:87

17. Red Squirrel   *Tamiasciurus hudsonicus fremonti* (Audubon & Bachman)
     1853. *Sciurus fremonti* Audubon & Bachman.   *The Viviparous Quadrupeds of North America*, 3(30): pl. 149, fig. 2; text, 3:237.

18. Red Squirrel   *Tamiasciurus hudsonicus lanuginosus* (Bachman)
     1839. *Sciurus lanuginosus* Bachman.   *Proc. Zool. Soc. London*, 1838:101.

19. Red Squirrel   *Tamiasciurus hudsonicus richardsonii* (Bachman)
     1839. *Sciurus richardsonii* Bachman.   *Proc. Zool. Soc. London*, 1838:100.

20. Douglas' Squirrel   *Tamiasciurus douglasii douglasii* (Bachman)
     1839. *Sciurus douglasii* Bachman.   *Proc. Zool. Soc. London*, 1838:99.

21. Douglas'Squirrel   *Tamiasciurus douglasii mollipilosus* (Audubon & Bachman)
     1841. *Sciurus mollipilosus* Audubon & Bachman.   *Proc. Acad. Nat. Sci. Philadelphia*, 1:102, October.

22. Northern Flying Squirrel   *Glaucomys sabrinus oregonensis* (Bachman)
     1839. *Pteromys oregonensis* Bachman.   *J. Acad. Nat. Sci. Philadelphia*, 8:101

23. Townsend's Pocket Gopher   *Thomomys townsendii townsendii* (Bachman)
     1839. *Geomys townsendii* Bachman. *J. Acad. Nat. Sci. Philadelphia,* 8:105.

24. Southeastern Pocket Gopher   *Geomys pinetis floridanus* (Audubon & Bachman)
     1853. *Pseudostoma floridanus* Audubon & Bachman. *The Viviparous Quadrupeds of North America,* 3:242.

* 25. Golden Mouse   *Ochrotomys nuttalli aureolus* (Audubon & Bachman)
     1841. *Mus (Calomys) aureolus* Audubon & Bachman. *Proc. Acad. Nat. Sci. Philadelphia,* 1:98.

26. Northern Grasshopper Mouse   *Onychomys leucogaster missouriensis* (Audubon & Bachman)
     1851. *Mus missouriensis* Audubon & Bachman. *The Viviparous Quadrupeds of North America,* 2:327.

* 27. Eastern Harvest Mouse   *Reithrodontomys humilis humilis* (Audubon & Bachman)
     1841. *Mus humilis* Audubon & Bachman. *Proc. Acad. Nat. Sci. Philadelphia,* 1:97.

28. Hispid Cotton Rat   *Sigmodon hispidus texianus* (Audubon & Bachman)
     1853. *Arvicola texiana* Audubon & Bachman. *The Viviparous Quadrupeds of North America,* 3:229.

29. Meadow Vole   *Microtus pennsylvanicus drummondii* (Audubon & Bachman)
     1853. *Arvicola drummondii* Audubon & Bachman. *The Viviparous Quadrupeds of North America,* 3:166.

30. Creeping Vole   *Microtus oregoni oregoni* (Bachman)
     1839. *Arvicola oregoni* Bachman. *J. Acad. Nat. Sci. Philadelphia,* 8(1):60.

31   Pine Vole   *Microtus pinetorum scalopsoides* (Audubon & Bachman)
     1841. *Arvicola scalopsoides* Audubon & Bachman. *Proc. Acad. Nat. Sci. Philadelphia,* 1:97, October.

* Original (or "type") specimen from South Carolina.

SILVER TRAY PRESENTED TO JOHN BACHMAN BY JOHN JAMES AUDUBON

Given to Bachman as a token of Audubon's esteem and gratitude. The motif was designed by Audubon.

Private Collection

"I would have liked to raise an everlasting monument, commemorating with a grand effect the history and portraits of the birds of America, by adding to each drawing of a single species a vignette exhibiting corresponding parts of the country where the specimen is most plentifully found; but having no taste for landscape-painting, and unable to employ a competent assistant for such a purpose, I with deep regret have relinquished the idea. I mention this to you, my dear friend, with hopes that at some future period some one better seconded by pecuniary means or talents may still engage in the undertaking. Sorry, notwithstanding, that as time flies Nature loses its primitiveness, and that pictures drawn in ten, or twenty, or more years, will no longer illustrate our delightful America pure from the hands of its Creator!"

JOHN JAMES AUDUBON, 1828, "Method of Drawing Birds," *Edinburgh Journal of Science*

PLATE 1   John James Audubon   Oil on canvas by John Woodhouse Audubon — *See Page 2*

PLATE 2   Chuck-Will's-Widow   Oil on canvas by John James Audubon — *See Page 17*

Sciurus hudsonius.

PLATE 3   **Red Squirrels**   Watercolor by John James Audubon — *See Page 100*

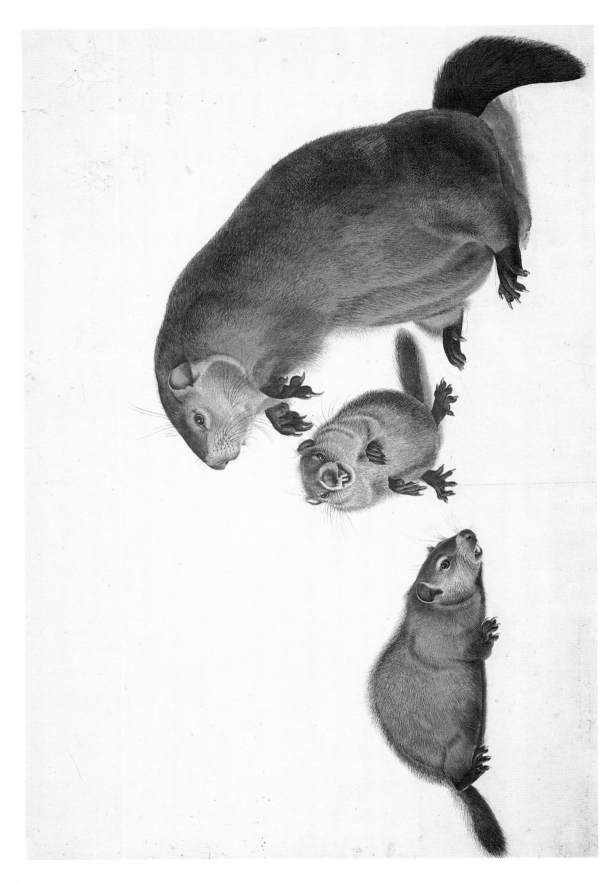

136

PLATE 4   Woodchucks

Watercolor by John James Audubon — *See Page 102*

Oil on canvas by Henry Jackson — *See Page 35*

PLATE 5   Bennett's Mill Pond

PLATE 6   John Bachman   Oil on canvas by John Woodhouse Audubon — *See Page 39*

PLATE 7 Bachman's Warbler   Plate 185, *The Birds of America — **See Page 46***

PLATE 8   Bachman's Sparrow   Plate 165, *The Birds of America* — ***See Page 44***

PLATE 9 Carolina Parakeet

Plate 26, *The Birds of America — See Page 90*

PLATE 10   White Peacock Butterfly   Watercolor by Maria Martin — *See Page 82*

PLATE 11   Snowy Egret   (S.C. rice plantation)   Plate 242, *The Birds of America* — *See Page 74*

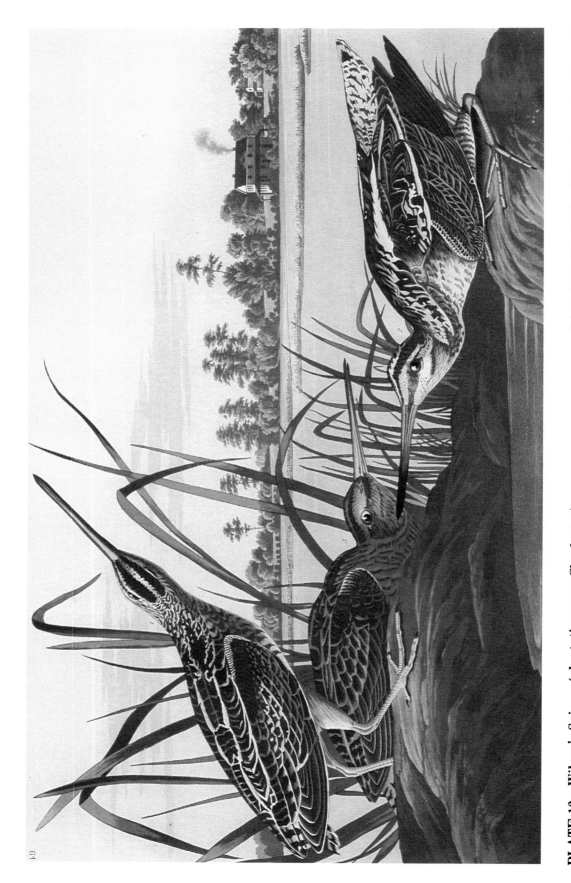

PLATE 12   Wilson's Snipe   (plantation near Charleston)

Plate 243, *The Birds of America* — *See Page 41*

PLATE 13   Lesser Yellowlegs   ("a few miles distant from Charleston")

Plate 288, *The Birds of America — See Page 43*

145

PLATE 14 Little Blue Heron (view near Charleston)

Plate 307, *The Birds of America* — *See Page 61*

PLATE 15 Long-billed Curlew (Charleston in background)

Plate 231, *The Birds of America* — *See Page 73*

147

PLATE 16 Rose Hill Plantation

Oil on canvas, artist not identified — *See Page 97*